THE TAROT AND THE MAGUS

OPENING THE KEY TO DIVINATION, MAGICK AND THE HOLY GUARDIAN ANGEL

Paul Hughes-Barlow is a practicing Magician and Tarot Reader. He regularly speaks at conferences and events, and has consulted to many journals and websites. He currently resides and practices in Brighton, England

AEON

THE TAROT AND THE MAGUS

OPENING THE KEY TO DIVINATION, MAGICK AND THE HOLY GUARDIAN ANGEL

Paul Hughes-Barlow

AEON

First published 2004
by Aeon Books Limited
London NW3

www.aeonbooks.co.uk

© Paul Hughes-Barlow 2004
The moral right of the author has been asserted

British Library Cataloguing in Publication Data

A C.I.P. is available for this book from the British Library

llustrations from Aleister Crowley Thoth Tarot® reproduced
by permission of AGM AGMüller. ©AGM AGMüller / OTO.

Extracts from the works of Aleister Crowley by permission of the OTO.

ISBN 978-1-90465-802-3

To Punditt Maharaj

Acknowledgements

Gérard Encausse, Éliphas Lévi, McGregor Mathers and Aleister Crowley, whose writings hint at many mysteries.

On the internet Jess Karlin and George Leake showed me the value of rigorous scholarship on the Tarot, while the email queries from tarot students around the world inspired me to create and develop the Tarot Lessons on Supertarot, the basis of this book.

My best inspiration comes from people not obviously associated with Tarot. Punditt's mysticism, teachings and spiritual help have always been forthcoming. Beryl's spiritual and inspirational help and faith in my abilities continues down the years, especially during the many dark days. Elayne gave me space and more to write in Houston Texas; the timely trip to New Orleans transformed the magical and spiritual direction of this book. Prospero provided mutual encouragement on writing books on Tarot in the various pubs of Kemptown. Last but not least, my Publisher who courageously allowed me to develop the book in ways beyond the original remits.

CONTENTS

Introduction

With hindsight it should have been obvious to all but the most shallow and incompetent magician that a book structured upon the Golden Dawn system of Tarot and the number eleven would inevitably result in some kind of magical or spiritual knowledge. However, the fact is that the original ambition was simply to present the Opening of the Key Spread, based upon the author's Supertarot website, to the general public. As the reader will see, this book is no mere primer on the subject of reading tarot cards.

There are many books on tarot decks in which the format is to present a picture of each card, provide a description and then to give the divinatory meanings. The format has changed little since A.E. Waite wrote the accompanying book to the Rider-Waite tarot nearly one hundred years ago. There are also a few books focussing on the many varieties of tarot spreads. This book is neither. The original intention was to study the first stage of the Opening of the Key Spread in which the cards are cut into four piles. The piles are turned over, the top cards analysed and then one of the piles is spread out in a horseshoe to be analysed using the Golden Dawn techniques of Pairing and Counting.

I have used this spread professionally for many, many years and promoted the spread on the Supertarot website. I not unnaturally considered myself fairly knowledgeable about this spread and was not expecting any surprises during the writing process. I could not have been more wrong. Since neither I nor the publisher wanted to create a book based upon the distinctly uninspiring formats currently followed, we hit upon the idea of structuring the book around eleven chapters, eleven being Aleister Crowley's favourite number of magick and change. The chapters would progressively move from Beginners to Advanced, with the later chapters devoted to more magical themes. Before the contract was signed, I asked my spiritual teacher for his blessing for writing this book, which was readily given, and he told me that 'Spirits would help me'. The first version, based upon the Supertarot website, was a failure. It would appear that I was not getting the spiritual assistance I was expecting. For a month, nothing was written. I was devoid of inspiration, until out of desperation I decided to base the book on Strings or sequences of cards, which are the basis of the Opening the Key Spread. On the face of it, this was more ambitious than the ideas found in Supertarot, but I found I could write easily and comfortably, and the deadline of three months looked attainable. The Spirits were helping me! When I was on the right track, ideas bubbled up from somewhere, and when I strayed, no matter how long I sat in front of the computer, not a word was written.

The Spirits seemed to be helping my Publisher too. It was his idea that I write a commentary on the paired Major cards at the beginning of each chapter. Frankly, I thought the idea preposterous, but since I was not getting anywhere, I gave it a try. Rather than compare and contrast the designs on the cards, an analysis of the gematria of the Hebrew letters associated with the cards seemed a good starting point. My expectations were zero, but remarkably the gematria produced relevant results that reflected on the character not only of the cards but the court cards and the Minor cards associated with the chapters, particularly when the divinatory meaning of three or four of a kind are considered. Nobody has ever come up with a satisfactory explanation for why the pictorial representations of the tarot are as they are, so perhaps we are closer to an answer.

Moreover, as I approached writing the pairings for the last few chapters, there came the dim realisation that I had been writing a grimoire. Quite what this grimoire represented, I had no real idea. Normally, grimoires usually provide various spiritual or magical solutions for problems, but this did not fit into that category. As a grimoire, it also focussed on the kabbalistic and gematriac values rather than Tarot per se, so I had nothing to go on. Besides, there was a book to write. The gematria values also threw light on why the Golden Dawn felt the need to transpose two of the cards. Without transposition, two identical gematria values occurred, which is clearly not acceptable. Since the Emperor and Star cards are naturally paired, Aleister Crowley's transposition of these cards makes not the slightest difference, and possibly points to an answer as to why there is still confusion as to the attributions of these cards.

Eleven is not a natural number as a means of analysis of the Tarot, which is probably why nobody has bothered before. Of course, individual cards can be analysed, such as the Fortune card, but it is not a fruitful topic in the bigger scheme of things. Multiplying 11 by that peculiarly sacred number of 7 comes to 77, one short. If we consider the Fool card to be zero, which it is, then in reality there are indeed 77 cards. Looking at the gematria (each hebrew letter is also a number and thus each hebrew word can be given a numerical value, see chart at the end of this Chapter) the values for 77 are far more inspiring than for 78. We have BOH, prayed, the river Gihon (Gen, ii, 13), Overflowing, Towers or Citadels, OZ meaning strength or a he-goat, and finally MZL, described as the influence from Kether, more commonly known as luck. It was not until the latter stages of writing this book that the the structure based upon 7 x 11 presented itself in the form of a new tarot spread that represents the modules or formulae of the structure of the Golden Dawn rituals. Although it is obvious that the Tarot is at the heart of the structure of the Golden Dawn rituals and teachings, I have for a long time been suspicious of the Pathworking relationships – there had to be other ways, one of which is the eleven steps relating to the General Exordium. The author has not had the time to fully explore the General Exordium in relationship to the Tarot, except to point out some possible avenues of exploration in to be found in the Meditations in Appendix I.

The author has always been of the opinion that there are 78 cards in a Tarot deck, despite several attempts to produce decks of 80 cards. New students of the Thoth tarot regularly ask why some versions of the decks have three Magus Cards, to which no satisfactory answer has been found, except to advise the student to discard two of the three Magi. The writing of this book has forced me to reconsider many sacred cows, as well as take a fresh look at older ideas. The fact is that approaching the Tarot from the direction of this book results in an extraordinary upsurge in creativity. Almost every day I get new ideas that could well go in another book on the Tarot. The possibilities are truly endless.

There are many innovations in this book. Although all the cards are discussed in some form, I have tried to take a sideways look at the cards, part of which comes from the inspiration of the Grimoire. As such, Aleister Crowley's *Book of Thoth* has been the prime source of inspiration, sometimes in relation to the Golden Dawn version. It has been the author's contention that the *Book of Thoth* is far closer to the precepts of the Golden Dawn than the so-called Golden Dawn Tarot decks, which contribute nothing to the genre. Crowley made genuine contributions to the Tarot, many of which have never been properly discussed. For example, why did he not name the deck the Tarot of Thelema? It was during the writing of this book that I unexpectedly got answers. I say unexpectedly because I have had questions like these for years and never gotten any answers.

Chapter 1 introduces the practicalities of the Opening of the Key Spread. The action of shuffling, dealing, counting and pairing is a ritual that helps the reader and Querent to be in a receptive state for the revelations that might appear.

Chapter 2 looks at the various ways of analysing the cards since the human brain is wired to see patterns. Since all 78 cards are used in a reading, divided into four piles, it is possible to look at the full representation of say all the fours, or the absence of a particular group of cards. One way of understanding this information is to look at the excess or absence of the sephiroth on the Tree of Life which gives a graphic representation of the dynamics of the String of cards, and should suggest magical balancing techniques to magicians at all levels. None of the techniques discussed are particularly part of the Golden Dawn techniques, but they serve as a means of engaging the reader into what could be going on. With practice, much of the analysis goes on at deeper levels of the psyche, allowing the conscious brain to get on with the dialogue that is part of the process of divination.

Chapter 3 looks at Pairing. The spiritual basis of Pairing is at the start of each chapter, but here we analyse the cards by pairing from the ends to the middle, and from individual cards. To pair is to create a polarity, a subject discussed by Dion Fortune in several of her books. Again, there are powerful spiritual and magical principles concealed in the Golden Dawn techniques of reading Tarot, which can be translated into magical practice.

In Chapter 4 we look at the use of Elemental Dignities. This is something that I have been battling to get accepted by the Tarot community for many years. The sad fact is that philosophy of any kind is not considered useful to understanding tarot, much to the detriment of divination, but the Golden Dawn divination ritual makes it abundantly clear that knowledge of the dialectic is fundamental to divination. The nature of the dialectic requires three elements, so we look at analysing cards in groups of three. Any discussion of the four elements is not complete without mentioning spirit, and there is evidence that some of the tarot cards should be seen as attributable to Spirit, rather than a particular element.

Now that there is an understanding of the relationship between two cards (Pairing), and three cards (Elemental Dignities), in Chapter 5 we leap not to four cards, which requires entirely different divination techniques, but to Strings of cards, where the order of cards to be interpreted is defined by the use of the Counting Technique.

Chapter 6 discusses a powerful development in the understanding of the nature of Strings. Some of the cards in a String are not counted, but it is not obvious which they are until all the cards are analysed. When these cards are understood to represent energies coming from elsewhere, such as a spiritual agency, then new possibilities of interpretation are possible.

Chapter 7 presents another reading that concerns that perennial favourite of tarot readings, love, and is a good example of how the Querent is interested in one person, but the Tarot presents other people who were not considered previously.

With Chapter 7, another reading that concerns that perennial favourite of tarot readings, love, and is a good example of how the Querent is interested in one person, but the Tarot presents other people who were not considered previously.

How one furnishes a room for ritual is vital. The same considerations apply for where the Tarot is read. In Chapter 8 I discuss ways of organising a room dedicated to the tarot, dealing with the public, and tackling that thorny problem of making predictions.

Chapter 9 marks the point where magical and spiritual techniques using the Tarot and the four elements are considered. Not everyone wishes to be a ceremonial magician, so Shamanism is an important viable alternative. One advantage of Shamanism is that it casts new light on the Celtic Cross Spread.

Chapter 10 looks at magic and spirituality from two apparently opposing directions. One the one hand, the practical basis of the Opening of the Key Spread can be found in the classic Kabbalistic text, the Sepher Yetsirah. The use of sex in magic in relationship to the Tarot and the Opening of the Key Spread is considered here.

In keeping with eleven being the number of transformation and change, the last chapter is dedicated to a discussion on the significance of the Aleister Crowley's Spirits of Liber 231 and the Goetia. In the latter stages of writing this book, these spirits gradually brought me to an understanding of the nature and role of the invocation of one's Holy Guardian Angel. The real significance of Pairing the Major Cards was brought home to me after I was shown the Eleven Stage tarot spread, named the Neophyte Spread.

At the beginnings of writing this book, I wrote an essay querying the title of the Opening of the Key Spread, and by the end I had the answer. The purpose of the Opening of the Key Spread is to enable the Magician to speak to his or her Holy Guardian Angel, through the offices of the Goetic and Liber 231 Spirits, and to understand the basis of all the Golden Dawn rituals to be based upon eleven. As ever, Crowley used and understood the nature of eleven, but it is now clear that he took the idea from the Golden Dawn. I start Chapter 1 with the Opening of the Key Spread, and the book finishes with the Neophyte Spread. Both use Elemental Dignities, Pairing and Counting.

Thus the book becomes a manual of high spiritual technique for safely contacting one's Holy Guardian Angel as well as a powerful methods of tarot divination. The promise of my teacher was kept, the spirits did help me in writing this book.

Numerical Values of the Hebrew Letters

Hebrew	Letter	Value
א	A	1
ב	B	2
ג	G	3
ד	D	4
ה	H	5
ו	V	6
ז	Z	7
ח	Ch	8
ט	T	9
י	Y	10
כ	K	20
ל	L	30
מ	M	40
נ	N	50
ס	S	60
ע	O	70
פ	P	80
צ	Tz	90
ק	Q	100
ר	R	200
ש	Sh	300
ת	Th	400

CHAPTER ONE

The Fool, The Universe and the Aces

0 The Fool = 1, Aleph
Air, Mother Letter

XXI The Universe = 400, Tau
Earth, Saturn, Double Letter

Naturally, these cards represent beginnings and endings. The Fool shows events happening from an unexpected source. The Universe is the matter in hand, the ending or completion of something or emigration to another country. Implicit in beginnings and endings is movement in time and place. Movement is from one Tree of Life to another, since the Fool starts with Kether and the Universe connects with Malkuth. Time can be from the past, present or future. A favourite saying in the Golden Dawn is that "Malkuth is Kether after another way".

The Fool is the first card, numbered Zero, while the Universe is the last, numbered 21. Kabbalistically, the Fool is Aleph, 1, while Malkuth is Tau, 400. In gematria 401 is the number of ATh, Essence, the thing itself, which is why, in divinatory matters, the Universe is the matter in hand. ATh also means with, at or near, whilst ThA means a room or a space defined by boundaries. Since Aleph and Tau represent the entire range of experience, we see that they define all 'rooms' from the subatomic to the largest galaxies.

The Book of Thoth says that, in mathematics, counting begins at zero and not one. Zero is also the final balance of opposites, a concept that runs through the Tarot. Zero or Nothing is not empty! Physicists tell us that the Zero Point teems with energy. Since the Fool card is AYN, Nothing is the source of all; it contains all the other 78 cards in seed form. Look at the Table of Contents in the Book of Thoth and you will see that the Fool card is unique in having its own section, while all the other 21 Major cards are lumped together. The Fool card also contains the form of the universe, a spiral or vortex, which is another concept that modern physics is starting to take more seriously.

The God of the Fool card, and therefore of the entire tarot deck, is surprisingly Dionysus, discoverer of the vine and wine. Divine inebriation is at the heart of the Greek Mysteries and Dionysus, the "Twice Born", represents the inner forces and divine potential within us all. Crowley only fleetingly mentions the pinecone held in the left hand of Dionysus in the Fool card. Another Golden Dawn adept, Dion Fortune, who wrote about Dionysus at the same time that Crowley was working on the Book of Thoth, describes the pine cone atop a

Maenad with Thyrsus

staff with tendrils of ivy or vine wound around as the thyrsus or magical weapon of Dionysus. The imagery parallels the Caduceus, discussed in Appendix B of the *Book of Thoth*, where the caduceus symbolises the chakras and kundalini energy. While discussion of the chakras and Kundalini is beyond the scope of this book, it is vital to understand that inner transformation precedes outer transformation and that some form of spiritual discipline is necessary, either in magical ritual, a lodge or yoga. The remarkable point is that Dionysus, the God of Tarot, unites the Thelemic system of Aleister Crowley, Dion Fortune's own magical system and Kundalini yoga!

An important key to understanding the Tarot is that this represents inner growth and spirituality as a means to touch the Divine within us all. Tarot is not about mere fortune telling – indeed Crowley in his letters insisted that his deck was not to be used for this purpose. Although I discuss how to read the Tarot for others, this book is not about fortune telling. It discusses the flows of energy within the Tarot cards that represent the situation the reading is about.

The energy flows are hard to describe. When sitting with a client, there is a slight change of awareness that corresponds to the situation either within or around the person. With practice, it becomes easier to understand and articulate those experiences. For example, I may feel quite blank or 'lost' and it turns out that the client has no idea of what direction to take or what to do with their lives. If I had less confidence in my abilities, I might have thought that the experience was my own and that I was not connecting to the client! The awareness is akin to a trance but again this is not something I am aware of so much until some disturbance. When I return my thoughts to the reading, I often have to ask the client where I had got to before being interrupted!

The energy flows are not the same as those experienced in the Meridians of Chinese philosophy or the Kundalini flow. However the Tarot cards do uniquely represent the situation in and around that person. If these energy flows are not right, they can be changed by the use of Will or Intent either by the Tarot reader or the client, in other words, by magic. If the energies are right but weak, the Will or intent of the Tarot reader or the client can enhance them. The chapters at the end of this book give more information on how this can be done. My experience is that working with the energies of the Tarot, using the techniques described below, brings about harmonisation between the inner energies and the outer energies.

Just as the Fool expresses the vacuum, the lightest aspect of Air, the Universe expresses the heaviest, most concrete form of matter, ruled by Saturn, the most constricted of the planets. Here we have the Principle of Polarity at its most extreme. Implicit within the Fool is the idea that Nothing contains Everything. In the Universe card Crowley chose to include the Periodic Table as a symbol of manifestation. While the Fool initiates the Great Work, the Universe represents the completion of the Great Work. Crowley says, "The Fool is the negative issuing into manifestation; the Universe is that manifestation, its purpose accomplished ready to return.... The image of the Universe in this sense is accordingly that of a maiden, the final letter of Tetragrammaton." (Book of Thoth), which links the Aces and Kether with the Princesses in Malkuth. As in the Fool card, the Universe depicts a spiral force that appears as if out of nowhere but here it is held by the maiden of the Tetragrammaton: "In her hands she manipulates the radiant spiral force, the active and the passive, each possessing its dual polarity." This spiral force is none other than the caduceus.

Between the Fool and the Universe are the twenty Major cards. We will examine their pairing at the beginning of each chapter.

The Ace of Wands Root of Fire

The Ace of Cups, Root of Water

The Ace of Swords, Root of Air

The Ace of Discs, Root of Earth

The Aces

The Aces are associated with Kether. KThR means Crown, something that is lowered onto the head. Again we have the suggestion of movement, of something lowered from above. Kether can be transposed to KRTh, cut off, again a sign of separation. Kether is associated with Atziluth or Nearness, another adjective which implies separation, but still relatively close. So while the Aces are about unity, in the Golden Dawn, they are "The Root of the Power of the Elements" implying that the Aces are not the Elements themselves but the beginnings of the Elements. The other implication of this statement is that the elements by themselves do not have any power unless connected to the Aces or Kether, rather like when the head is cut off from the body. By definition, roots are hidden. The Aces are separate from the rest of the Minor cards – they are more at home with the Court cards while the rest of the 36 Minor cards are associated with the Decanate system of astrology.

Two Aces in a String usually suggest a move of home or work
Three Aces indicate re-organisation, so I suggest clearing out the house, feng
    shui style.
Four Aces represent great power.

Since all elements are in their root form, the Aces represent Spirit and the four elements, representing Osiris, spirituality, in the Golden Dawn system. The presence of all four elements represents balance and harmony, the rule of law and great power. The Opening of the Key Tarot spread starts by having all 78 cards cut into four piles – no cards are missing and they come under the rule of the element of that pile. In later chapters of this book, the evocation of spirits depends on the thorough analysis of all 78 cards and essential checks and balances to provide the balanced energies required for the spirits to appear.

The Aces represent the four quarters around the North Pole, with the Meridian running through the Great Pyramid at Giza eastwards. The Fire Ace covers Asia, Water the Pacific, Air the Americas and Earth for Europe and Africa. In the *Book of Thoth*, the Aces "... form a link between the small cards and the Princesses who rule the Heavens around the North Pole". This remarkable statement projects the Tarot from being something about the petty concerns of the individual into a grand arena that unites the individual with the ancient past, the Pyramids, the concept of time – the Precession of the Equinoxes, out into the entire Universe.

The Aces have no astrological attributions – they are timeless, therefore balanced Spiritual power is the key to transforming time.

The Opening of the Key Spread

The Opening of the Key Spread (OOTK) is the crowning glory of the Golden Dawn system of Magic. It is almost virgin territory that is crying out to be explored. The five stages of the Spread are intimidating in themselves, since they require the Tarot reader to be familiar with the four elements, astrology, Kabbalah and Enochian Magick; a tall order even for experienced magicians. However, common to all five stages are the fundamental techniques of Pairing, Counting and Elemental Dignities (ED's) - every stage requires them. Familiarity with these techniques will enable the Tarot reader to successfully work through the entire five stages without an in-depth knowledge of astrology and Kabbalah.

Most Tarot spreads are positional in that the reader places usually one card on a number of positions that are related to concepts such as past, present, future, health, friendship, love and work. Interpretation relies on remembering the divinatory meanings of the card and then relating that meaning to the position in question.

Tarot readers therefore have a lot of problems to overcome. One card on one position creates a kind of equivalence that is supposed to equate with life. However a moment's thought should convince you that this is not a likely prospect. It is very rare for an individual to have a healthy balance between concepts. The nature of modern life demands imbalance – very often social contact and love life revolves around the workplace. There is also a problem in seeing how only a select few cards can represent the life of an individual.

In contrast, The Opening of the Key Spread utilises the entire 78 cards, divided into four piles. My experience of using this spread professionally to the public is that even when told to "cut the cards in half", the client will cut the cards almost anywhere! The piles are then cut in half again to create four piles. The Golden Dawn Adept would have cut four equal piles, but I invariably end up having to interpret a representation of Manhattan. This is actually a distinct advantage since I know roughly what those four piles represent. Simply by inspection of the relative heights of the piles, an impression can be gained of relative excesses and lacks in the life of the client. I am not astonished at seeing the third pile, related to Air and problems, being the highest. A very small Water pile can show lack of love or emotion, while a large Fire pile can indicate excess activity but can also show an obsession with the past. A small Earth pile perhaps shows lack of faith in the future.

We will discuss methods of interpreting the Tarot using patterns in the Opening of the Key spread, but in the chapters that follow I will present tarot spreads that you can use as an exercise to improve your divinatory skills using Elemental Dignities.

Elemental is a word that first appeared in the 15th century. It means "relating or being the basic or essential constituent of something", and also relates to "great forces of nature" such as a storm. Elemental represents first principles and primary ingredients, the four elements; Fire, Water, Air and Earth.

Dignity bestows honour on the elements:
1. The quality or state of being worthy of esteem or respect.
2. Inherent nobility and worth: *the dignity of honest labor.*
3. Poise and self-respect.
4. Stateliness and formality in manner and appearance.
5. The respect and honor associated with an important position.
6. A high office or rank.
7. **Dignities** The ceremonial symbols and observances attached to high office.

As well as the concept of relatedness and a sense of hierarchy, Dignity gives the means for elevation. We see that, within the context of the Opening of the Key Spread, the use of Elemental Dignities in balancing and analysing the elements gives rise to the ability to transcend or go beyond one's situation.

The book focuses on the Pairing, Counting and Elemental Dignity techniques used in a real reading for the first Stage of the Opening of the Key Spread. I normally would work systematically through all four Piles of cards corresponding to the four elements, analysing each card in terms of Elemental Dignities as they were paired and counted. However, such an approach is tedious to the reader, so I will only analyse the Fire Pile in depth.

The method of laying out cards in this and the following chapters is entirely different from almost all other spreads, in which the number of positions and the number of cards on each position is predetermined. In exercises (and in readings where you do not have the time or inclination to perform a full reading), the simplest method is to shuffle the cards, arbitrarily cut the deck, and read the cards. The largest String size can be approximately thirty cards and the smallest can be as low as seven

The Opening of the Key Spread has its own method of cutting the cards. Shuffle the cards and place the deck to your right.

L   □   *R*

Cut the deck approximately in half and place to the left of the original pile, leaving enough space to put more cards between them.

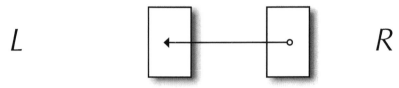

Cut the right hand pile approximately in half and place between the two piles.

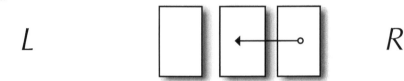

Take the far left pile, cut it in half and place to the left. You will now have four piles of cards.

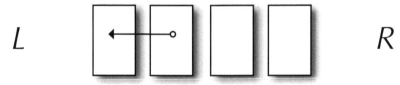

Turn the piles over and interpret the top cards using Elemental Dignities and any other appropriate method.

One of the piles is selected and analysed. In this book, the Fire pile (the first pile on the right) is spread out and analysed. Note that the cards are fanned out with the top card to the right. If the reader is using the Book of Thoth, the use of colour enables the cards to be read even when most of them are obscured, something that is not possible with Rider-Waite tarot decks.

Chapter Two

The Magus, The Aeon, the Twos and the Knights

I The Magus = 2, Beth
Air, Mercury, Double Letter

XX The Aeon = 300, Shin
Fire, Mother Letter

The Magus represents Mercury, communication and control: he has four weapons representing the four elements. In the same way that the Aces are the powers of the elements but not the elements themselves, the Two's show the four elements in their pure state. The Magus organises and the Aeon shows movement from the present with respect to the past, or a new current with respect to the future.

We have time represented as past, present and future contrasting with the previous pairing of Fool and Universe in which space is defined. Chokmah is the symbol of the Father and so the Knights are associated with this Sephirah. Beth and Shin total 302, the number of ARQA, Earth, and QBR is a cave, a hole in the Earth or a tomb. RQB means 'to putrefy'; the Judgment card traditionally is associated with tombs and resurrection. A subtler interpretation of RQB is tied to the notion of the birth of the pure elements at the level of Chokmah. They represent a descent into matter and therefore are not pure. As soon as the elements appear, they will degrade, reflecting the astrological attributes of Cardinal, Fixed and Mutability of the 12 signs of the zodiac.

The Magus holds a baton or Wand that represents energy sent forth from Kether; obvious phallic imagery. Within the Supernal Triangle, we deal in paradoxes. Crowley tells us that the Magus is "... the Word of creation whose speech is silence". The Magus represents truth and falsehood, wisdom and folly, since his energy has not been shaped through the forming power of Binah nor has he reached the knowledge of Daath. Crowley mentions the lemniscate or symbol of infinity in relation to the Magus. It also appears on the 2 of Disks showing that he may well have used this method of pairing as inspiration. Some versions of the Book of Thoth contain three versions of the Magus card – two of them should be removed for divination purposes.

The Book of Thoth departs from the traditional view of the Angels of Judgment. A new era started in 1904 for Crowley when "the fiery god Horus takes over from the airy god Osiris in the East as Hierophant". Even though the Hierophant is associated with the Earth and Taurus, it is the first graphic to appear in the Book of Thoth. The Stélé of Revealing is intimately associated with the Aeon because it was the inspiration for the reception of the Book of the Law.

The dualistic nature of the Aeon is brought out in Crowley's description of the brothers Ra-Hoor-khuit and Hoor-pa-kraat, which parallels the qualities of the Magus card. The Path on the Tree of Life for the Aeon is between Malkuth and Hod. We see Crowley has paired the Aeon card with the Magus, even down to the appropriation of the Solar energies to both cards. This insight casts new light on the verse from the Book of the Law quoted in the commentary: "I am the Lord of the Double Wand of Power; the wand of the Force of Coph Nia; but my left hand is empty, for I have crushed an Universe; & nought remains". There are obvious references to the previous cards Fool and Universe and the Wand of the Magus has become the "Double Wand of Power".

In these two cards we see a cycle of creation emanating from the Magus then destroyed by the Lord of the Aeon. The question of what is created and destroyed is answered in the commentary on the Magus card – the four elements. The Magus shows discrimination – he has arranged the four elemental weapons on the altar, while the Aeon card simply destroys everything in its path either as in Shiva, or the ending of a cycle.

While the Aces show the Roots of the Powers of the Elements, the Two's represent the elements in their pure form. In the context of the Magus and Aeon cards, we see that at this level of purity, the elements are being constantly created and destroyed. This is reinforced by the use of the symbol of infinity and by the transient, impermanent nature of the Knights on horseback that represent the Yods in YHVH.

The Two's

The elements appear in their pure form in the Two's. They are associated with Chokmah and mark the beginning of the decanates of astrology. Three two's indicate reorganization or recommencement of a project from the past (Judgment, Aeon) while four two's indicate conferences or conversations (Magus).

2 Wands – Lord of Dominion

A dictionary definition of Dominion is:

1: obsolete: supreme excellence or an example of it

2a: supreme power especially over a body politic b: freedom from external
    control: AUTONOMY c: controlling influence

3: one that is sovereign; especially : an autonomous state

The definitions highlight the concept that the elements are above all and cannot be influenced. The transiency of the elements – the way they are continually made and destroyed - ensures that no repeatable patterns emerge for control to be exerted on them. Dominion does not mean subjugation! The Golden Dawn title is recursive in the obsolete definition. The autonomy of rule represented by the 2 Wands is forever but of course there is no sense of permanency – at any time we can rise beyond the elements and make the elements work for us. Dominion is also an Order of Angel. The sign of Aries, where this card starts, is notorious for beginning things but not completion. The continual state of change required is supplied by the 2 Disks.

2 Cups – Lord of Love

The 2 Wands has dominion and it never had to conquer – what is there to conquer except itself? It conquers itself by continual change, not subjugation. Since no external force can be applied and there is no danger of dissent, Love rules easily and naturally. Things can stay the same. The elements are united in attraction.

2 Swords – Lord of Peace

Crowley's insight shines out as he states "the Two of Swords was formerly called the Lord of Peace Restored; but this word "restored" is incorrect because there has been no disturbance". Peace rules because the elements are harmonious within themselves and autocratic beyond the petty corruptions of daily life.

2 Disks – Lord of Change

The Golden Dawn title "Lord of Harmonious Change" shows redundancy of language. It is sufficient to understand the exalted levels at which the Elements remain in their pure state, being continually created and destroyed in order to maintain their Dominion over creation. As Crowley says *"Earth is the throne of Spirit; having got to the bottom, one immediately comes out again at the top. Hence, the card manifests the symbolism of the serpent of the endless band"*.

The Knights

The four Knights show swift moving events, the birth of the elements while three Knights show news or unexpected meetings, a quality of Mercury. The Knights represent the fiery part of YHVH, the action is quick and violent but does not last. In the same way the Two's represent the Decanates and Chokmah on the Tree of Life, the Knights also represent the rule of the Celestial regions. The swirling energy of Chokmah is represented as the zodiac at the mundane level and with the Ophanim, the Angelic order of Wheels. In his analysis of the Knights, Crowley says it is important to understand "...the correspondences between the Symbol and the Natural Forces which they represent; and it is essential to practical Magical work to have assimilated this knowledge". The Knights are part of the Supernal Triangle.

Knight of Wands, Lord of Flame and Lightning

Lightning is the most transient manifestation of Fire. Crowley's divinatory advice is to not to rush but to be calm and considerate, which is in harmony with the advice from the I Ching on Hexagram 51, The Arousing, Shock, Thunder. Why all this timidity? In his pure state the Knight, in a state of grace in Chokmah, already has Dominion, so why should he go anywhere else?

Knight of Cups, Lord of Rain and Springs

The Golden Dawn calls him the Lord of the Waves and the Waters. Waves are created by the movement of Air, which does not figure yet in the analysis. Rain appears during thunderstorms. You might think that words like 'aggression' would be associated with the Knight of Wands but it appears here. Perhaps the qualities of passive aggression are being suggested. The fiery aspect of water is suggested by the use of 'brilliance' and 'fluorescence'. Crowley mentions the power of solution, the ability to dissolve, echoing the alchemic motto *solve et coagula* which appears in the Art card. The ability to dissolve substances in solution is enhanced when the liquid is heated.

Knight of Swords, Lord of the Wind and Storm

The Golden Dawn title is Lord of Wind and Breezes but Crowley sees greater violence. This Knight represents the idea of attack. Since we are looking at the highest principles of Tarot, we can do no better than Zoroaster, frequently mentioned in the Book of Thoth. It is described as 'the True Will exploding the mind spontaneously'. Most of us would take some time to prepare for such an eventuality.

Knight of Disks, Lord of the wide and fertile Land

The title is not a description of Fire of Earth, which refers to mountains, earthquakes and volcanoes. Crowley includes gravitation, presumably referring to forces (fire) acting through objects (earth). The picture of the Knight is largely agrarian, representing fertile land that provides for the people. Remember that the Knights have not indulged in any action, since they are in the Dominion of Chokmah. The 2 Disks, Change, may possibly refer to the cycle of the seasons worked by the Knight.

Overview of Reading the Cards

Basic Strings

In this book we have Strings of cards rather than positions for cards in a reading that correspond to the Past, Present, Future, Health, Work, Love, etc (The Celtic Cross Spread is a good example). The length of a String can vary from around five or six cards to over thirty. Rather than impose an arbitrary meaning on each position, the topic of a string not only depends on the cards in the string, but also on the position and relationship of the cards to each other. It is possible, albeit rather impractical, to read the entire string of 78 cards. The next four Chapters discuss various ways of analysing these strings.

Topics can have sub-topics and so we find a similar thing happening in the Strings. The grouping of cards may suggest sub-topics that can be analysed separately within the full String, but it is important to note that once the cards have been cut into the various piles the order of the String of cards is not changed. This is very important. If Reversed cards are permitted they should not be altered either.

The Examples of Strings in this book were taken from a real reading. The cards were cut into four piles by the Client using the Golden Dawn method of the Opening of the Key Tarot Spread. The original reading took about half an hour and of course was not as detailed as described in the following chapters. The Client is a regular visitor and she confirmed to me that the extra detail in this book corresponds to events that actually happened.

We are not concerned with individual meanings of the cards but how they relate to each other. Any imbalances found in one String may be balanced by the makeup of one of the other three Strings. The four Strings follow the YHVH order - Fire, Water, Air and Earth. However, for reasons of brevity in this volume we will only examine the Fire String in detail.

The methods of seeing the bigger picture that I apply to each String are:

- Top Card (Overview)
- Number of Cards (Relates to the cardinal numbering of a Major card)
- Centre card or pair of cards
- Major/Minor/Court Cards imbalance
- Three or Four of a kind
- Tree of Life
- Reversals
- Elemental imbalance

Tarot readers will find with experience that not all of these methods are relevant, neither is it necessary to use them all. However, as we will see, combination of the methods helps to confirm the picture we build up of the reading and our own intuition. The reader does not have to follow the order I suggest either – you may have your own ideas about what these or other categories mean in a reading, or you may develop your own categories and interpretations.

Sometimes it is hard to get into a reading and we need ways such as these to get going. Once started, momentum can be gained easily and there is more fluency as we speak. The key phrases suggested by these methods can trigger something in the mind of the querent that helps the reading to work smoothly to generate the dialogue that is required for a successful reading.

Although I have entitled this chapter 'Basic Strings', there is an incredible richness and subtlety arising from the techniques, as we shall see.

Top Card

The interpretation of the top card is the general Divinatory Meaning (DM), providing an overview of what the more elaborate reading of all the cards will disclose. There are times when the top cards can be used for really quick readings.

Number of Cards

The number of cards in the String can be used to indicate the hidden influence of a Major card that may be in one of the other Strings. If the number is 22 or less, we can easily attribute the entire String to one of the Major cards; if there are more than 22, subtract 22 from the number of cards and use the result to assign it to a Major card. The Fool is assigned to Zero so it is the first card and the Magus is second and so on. The number of the Major card is one less than the number of cards in the reading. If there were 14 cards, we would relate to the Death card. If we had 26 cards, then the remaining 4 would indicate the Empress. If that Major card is in the String, we can assign greater significance to it or we can look to see where that card appears in the other Strings and interpret accordingly.

Centre card or pair of cards

If the total number of cards in a String is odd, there will be a centre card and if the number of cards is even, there will be a pair of cards at the centre. Odd numbers are more decisive, they show a resolution, rather than a choice. If the top card gives the overview, the Centre card shows the outcome. Again we have a quick method of interpretation when time is at a premium.

Major/Minor/Court Cards balance

As a rule of thumb, in any String with a balanced distribution of cards, half the cards will be Minor, while Court cards and Major cards will comprise the other half. There will be one or two more Major cards than Court cards. Strings of 12 cards or fewer often show extremes but this is not as significant as when extremes are present in larger Strings of 20 cards or more. If the cards are cut into four equal Strings, there should be approximately 19 or 20 cards, which translate into 10 or 11 Minor cards and 5 or 6 Major and Court cards.

An excess of Major cards indicates that the Querent may feel that he is not in control of his life or that there is a sense of fatalism. Excess Court cards shows that too many people are interfering in the life of the Querent. Excess Minor cards show that the Querent is either entirely in control of the situation and is not relying on Fate (Major Cards) or the assistance of other people (Court cards), or it may indicate that the Querent is a control freak.

Three or Four of a Kind

The next two categories can be related to each other in terms of the Sephiroth on the Tree of Life. The nature of Three or Four of a kind has been established for over a century, but the origins of these interpretations are obscure. In the Meditation at the beginning of each Chapter, the relevant interpretations have been included. The origins may lie in the Gematria of the Paired Major cards when the Minor cards and Court cards of the relevant Sephirah are included.

Groups of three or four of a kind have special meanings that give an extra insight and suggested interpretations are found in the Meditation at the beginnings of the chapters.

Tree of Life

Missing numbers indicate a lack that may or may not need to be fulfilled by the placement of the missing cards in the other Strings. The interpretations are speculative, but we can consider them to be the lack of what four of a kind would represent. The larger the number of cards in a String, the more significant any omissions will be.

The information can be used to see if particular parts of the Tree of Life are missing. The Pillar of Severity is composed of the 3's, 5's and 8's. The lack of 3's and 5's would indicate a weak Pillar of Severity suggesting that the Querent is not controlling what is going on around him or her. This may manifest as aggression in communication (the 8's) to compensate. How many people rant and rave when they do not get their own way in life?

In the Middle Pillar, the omission of a large part of the Aces, 6's, 9's and 10's would suggest massive mood swings or that life alternates between aggression and passivity. The Pillar of Mercy contains the 2's, 4's, and 7's and an absence of some of these numbers will indicate that the querent feels under attack or insecure in his life. The remaining 2, 4 or 7 available are seen as rocks to cling on to.

The concept can be extended to the Triangles. If the Supernal Triangle (1, 2, 3) was weak or non-existent, there would be a feeling of being disconnected or separate from the parents (2 represents the Father, while 3 is the Mother). Such feelings are directed through any Knight or Queen cards present.

An absent or weak Ethical Triangle (4, 5, 6) could indicate some kind of amorality or criminality, perhaps channelled through any Princes in the String. If the Astral Triangle (7, 8, 9) is weak or missing there could be problems with emotional immaturity (7), inability to communicate (8), or feelings of disconnection with people (9). You may include the 10's in analysis of the Astral Triangle, in which case the Princesses would come into play.

In all cases, the cards that are present have to compensate for the missing cards, pointing to behavioural imbalance. Study of the other Strings in which those cards are found may give clues about appropriate advice. If you are familiar with the Tree of Life, you may also look to the Major cards that connect the Sephiroth. For example, if the Lust card is present, but the 4's and 5's are absent, it would be as if the fetters have been removed from this card, leading it to act in a totally indulgent manner without concern for the thoughts and feelings of others. Conversely, if the Lust card were absent from the String, but all four 4's and 5's were present, the flow between them would be blocked, and there may be inhibition about that card wherever it is found in the other Strings.

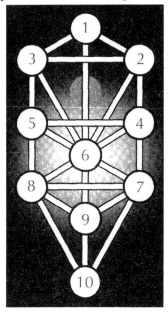

The Tree of Life

The question arises concerning missing Sephiroth that are not connected, such as Binah and Yesod. There are systems that connect these 'invisible' paths using the Court cards. Of course, there will be no Major card to connect them but in this example, we have the Saturn and Lunar aspects missing suggesting a lack of feminine influence in the life of the Querent. Another approach is to look at the natal chart to check the aspect strength or lack between Saturn and the Moon.

Reversals

With Tarot spreads that have one card for each position, there is a tendency to see reversed cards as having a negative connotation or that the divinatory meaning (DM) is somehow reversed. With Strings, we can see groups of reversals indicating just that – another method of grouping the cards. This is useful when there are only two court cards and one of them is reversed. We might see the reversed cards associated with the reversed Court card, even if there appears to be no other connection. The bottom line is to use the reversed meanings for cards only when appropriate. As in life, there are many shades of grey; using these techniques gives us the choice of when and where we use them.

Elemental Imbalances

In the Tarot, the Wands represent Fire, the Cups represent Water, the Swords are Air, and the Disks or Pentacles are Earth. The elemental balance of the Minor and Court cards is therefore easy to calculate. The elemental attributions of the Major cards are based upon the Sephirah Yetsirah

A majority of Fire cards shows energy, opposition or a quarrel. An excess of Water cards show pleasure, fun or romance. An excess of Air cards shows trouble, sadness, illness or death, and an excess of Earth cards shows a concentration on business, finances or possessions.

Missing or low levels of an element show where the querent has a corresponding lack in the same areas. A balancing excess of that element may be found in one of the other Strings, which the Querent may or may not be aware of.

The Fire String

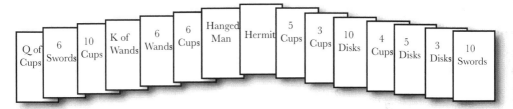

Top Card - 10 Swords. This card signifies Ruin, weakness or corruption.

Number of Cards - Fifteen cards suggests the Art or Temperance card, which signifies a combination of forces searching for the means to escape, or complex ways of doing things, as opposed to simple and straightforward means.

Centre Card - The Hermit shows the desire for solitude, or hidden forces at work, as the likely outcome.

Major/Minor/Court - With only two each of the Major and Court cards out of the fifteen, there is a massive imbalance towards individual effort – don't expect an external event to change the circumstances. A more balanced distribution would have been 8 Minor cards, 4 Major cards, and 3 Court cards.

Three or Four of a kind - Three 6's show success and gain and three 10's indicate buying, selling and commerce.

Tree of Life - There are no Aces, Two's, Sevens, Eights or Nines. In terms of the Tree of Life, the triangle from Netzach, Hod and Yesod is missing. The weak Supernal Triangle suggests feelings of isolation or lack of parental role for which the Court cards are trying to compensate in their own life. The absence of the Astral triangle indicates the problems of expressing thoughts and feelings. Perhaps the Knight and Queen in this String are trying to avoid the mistakes of their parents (Supernal Triangle), pretending (no Astral Triangle) that everything is fine (three 6's), or compensating by spending money (three 10's). The missing 8's and 9's are found in the Air String (problems and worries), while three 7's reside in the Earth String (the outcome). The Major cards associated with paths between the missing sephiroth are:

Fool $(1 - 2)$
Tower $(7 - 8)$
Sun $(8 - 9)$
Emperor $(7 - 9)$

All four cards have a strong masculine component suggesting a lack of leadership that reinforces the passivity indicated by the majority of water cards. Although there are no 2's, Knights traditionally represent Chokmah but of course the functions of the 2's and Knights are different. If we substituted the Knight for the lack of 2's, then the Fool would not be significant. For the Knight to function in this manner is merely a sticking plaster over a gaping wound and he would indeed be acting in a foolish manner, even if only as far as the Queen is concerned.

Reversals - Of the two court cards, the Queen is reversed whilst the Knight is the normal way up. The Queen is at the centre of six reversed cards and the

Knight can be seen as one normal card amidst a total of nine reversed cards suggesting that she is calling the shots. In fact, nine of the fifteen cards are reversed.

Elements - Water is the dominating element and, with the Earth cards, there are eleven passive to four active cards. There are only two each of the Fire and Air cards, indicating how little movement is happening in the fire pile – the Fire cards are the Knight and 6 Wands and we already have evidence in the Reversals that the Queen is in control.

Summary - We can summarise the cards so far as arguments (10 Swords) between two people (Queen and Knight) caused by their own efforts (excess Minor cards and no other Court Cards). There are a lot of emotional upsets (excess water) possibly about money (Disks) creating a passive situation (Earth and Water dominate), in which they pretend the problems do not exist (three 6's) or spend money (three 10's) to compensate. The situation may be made more complex (Art/Temperance) as a way of not tackling the issues and one of the court cards wants to be alone (Hermit). If the couple have split up, either they have not resolved these issues or they want to bury them (Death). The absence of the Astral Triangle points to communication problems. The weak Supernal Triangle possibly points to problems from the way they were treated by their parents that are not inflicted on their own children.

Another way of summarising the String is as follows: a relationship is in ruins (10 Swords), due to action or inaction (excess Minor cards). The situation has the appearance of stability, particularly financial security (6's and 10's). However, the absence of the Astral Triangle indicates that the couple have not developed the ability to use their imagination to create the lives that they desire. Although water is the dominant element, emotions are being held in check. It is the Queen who is keeping the situation locked, not wanting to lose stability. Temperance/Art and the Hermit suggest that the couple spend time resolving their individual issues, so that the change suggested by the Five of Theosophic Reduction and the missing 5 of the Minor cards and the missing Major cards (Tower, Sun, and Emperor) can occur. When change happens it will be radical, deep and transforming.

As you can see, even without any kind of in-depth analysis of individual cards, it is possible to get a feel for what the reading is about. For practice, try doing a reading by laying out four Strings of cards of varying sizes and looking for common themes.

Although the techniques are described as 'basic', do not underestimate their power. There are times when even a superficial analysis of the cards leads the Tarot Reader to the right conclusion, even when time is precious. The advanced techniques of Card Counting analysis require in-depth knowledge of these methods, particularly when a magical ritual is being contemplated. Some of the methods require study of the Tree of Life, but these are methods that do not seem to work so well when reading a tarot spread based upon the Tree of Life, since we are looking at absence, not just presence. Just as car drivers find themselves at home without ever remembering anything of the journey, the ritual of cutting the cards into the four piles, the turning over of the four piles and the spreading out of the cards begin to work at deeper and deeper levels of the mind. Simply by scanning over the cards, something magical happens. Within levels of awareness not only of the Reader, but also of the Client, there is the experience of flows of energy that transform through the reading. Sometimes the energy is focussed, then it flows, returns, finds blockages or dithers and sometimes results in visions that are greater than the sum of the contents of the individual cards.

CHAPTER THREE

The Priestess, The Sun, the Threes and the Queens

II The Priestess = 3. Gimel
Water, Moon, Double Letter

XIX The Sun = 200, Resh
Fire, Sun, Double Letter

The Threes are part of the Supernal Triangle. The High Priestess is on the only path that goes from Kether to the Tree of Life below the abyss. The Priestess also represents the Moon partner to the Sun and the path of the Priestess is from Kether the Crown to Tipareth the Sun.

The numeration of these two cards is 203 – ABR, passed away, feather (symbol of Maat), wing, genitalia. ARB means to lie in wait. BAR is a well or spring and BRA means Created, the root of the word Briah, the watery second level of creation after Atziluth, associated with Chokmah and Binah. The Feather or Wing evokes Air, which came from Kether and in particular the Fool card, as well as the symbol of the Goddess Maat.

We have masculine and feminine images here. Kabbalistically, Binah is the Great Mother and the image is of the Dark Sea. Venus would be the obvious planet to associate with it but actually it is Saturn. ABR is also lead, the metal of Binah. GR means dwelling or abiding or a stranger, foreigner, pilgrim or guest. Chokmah and Binah together represent the watery and creative level of Briah. The Queens are usually depicted on a Throne, another symbol of Binah.

The pairing of the High Priestess and the Sun represents the natural pairing of the Sun and the Moon. Unlike the Fool or the Magus, which both remain in the Supernal Triangle, the Priestess descends vertically across the Abyss to Tipareth, the natural Sephiroth of the Sun. She connects the Father in Kether to the Son in Tipareth. For Crowley, the Priestess represents AYN SVP AVR, or limitless light, and since we know the Fool as Zero is AYN, then the Magus is AYN SVP. The High Priestess represents the illumination of Light from Kether, which we would not otherwise see, since Kether is cut off from the rest of the tree. As Light, she balances the energies of the Fool and Magus. Everything about the High Priestess is potentiality. For those who attain the level of Tipareth and hear the voice of their own Holy Guardian Angel, it will be Hers.

The Sun is another card concerning Light, but here there has already been manifestation and differentiation – we see children, the twins who appear in the Aeon card. While the Priestess indicates potentiality, here we have form, we have the earth built into a mound and around this mound there is a wall, and there is the zodiac. The Priestess represents Isis, the Eternal Virgin and Artemis, the Hunter, while the Sun represents Nuith who is "one girdle of Our Lady of infinite space" (Isis). The Sun represents the transition from one Age to another, while the Camel in the High Priestess continues its long and lonely journey across the desert and the chaos of the Abyss.

The Three's

3 Threes indicate deceit or deception, referring to the illusory quality of Briah.

4 threes is a sign of determination, possibly referring to the determination to travel through the desert on a Camel (Priestess) in the blazing heat (Sun).

Since the Three's are in Binah, part of the Supernal Triangle, there is very little differentiation between the cards. The formulation of the Triangle represents the fertilized idea: "In each case, the idea is of a certain stability which can never be upset, but from which a child can issue".

3 Wands, Lord of Virtue

This card is the product of the Ace and 2 Wands, whose will and dominion suggests integrity. "The mother conceives, prepares and gives birth to its manifestation".

3 Cups Lord of Abundance

The product of love is abundance. Crowley sees Demeter or Persephone, who find their fulfilment in the Princess of Disks. Abundance should be enjoyed but beware of attachment to the fruits.

3 Swords Lord of Sorrow

The dire divinatory meaning of misery, separation and illness does not have as much force when we see this card in the context of the Supernal Triangle. It becomes the Mourning of Isis, the quality of melancholy, the

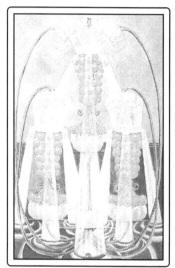

darkness of the Great Sea. The desire to create seems to have been perverted – "… its children are monsters".

3 Disks Lord of Work

This card represents the crystallization of forces – something has definitely been done. The 3 Disks never stops

working – it is continual, symbolised by the three gunas and the three Mother Letters, which are discussed fully in the Fortune card.

The Queens

The two Major cards here deal with Light in different aspects, yet the third Sephirah Binah is the place of the Dark Sea, the colour of Binah is Black, and the magical symbol is of a mature woman or matron, and of course Binah derives itself from the reception of energy from Chokmah, not Kether. The Queens are seated on Thrones, indicating the influence of Binah in the Supernal Triangle.

Four Queens indicate authority and influence.

Three Queens show friends in high places.

Queen of the Thrones of Flame

The Queen is seated on flames. Her Wand is topped with a cone symbolising the mysteries of Bacchus that relate to the Fool. Crowley characterises this woman as having contrary qualities.

Queen of the Thrones of the Waters

The watery part of water is symbolised by the qualities of the Great Mother and Isis. The endless curves of light are geometric forms from Rudolf Steiner's projective synthetic geometry. The characteristics of the queen tend to reflect the influences upon her.

Queen of Thrones of Air

The upper part of her body is naked, which represents her being this side of the veil. The child's head on her helmet relates to the position of Tipareth. She represents liberation of the Mind.

Queen of Thrones of Earth

The Queen brings fertility and water to arid regions, as such she symbolises both the Great Work (meeting one's Holy Guardian Angel') and the Great Work of Creation. The sceptre appears to have a hexagram, but it is a cube containing a three dimensional Hexagram, which must have taxed the artistic abilities of Frieda Harris. The spiral horns symbolise the process of Creation.

Pairing the Cards

We have looked at the String of cards in a general form and now we can use Pairing to build up a story of what might be going on in the reading. This is an actual Golden Dawn Tarot technique which is a powerful system of magic in itself.

The technique involves pairing the cards at the extremities of the String, moving to the centre. The next pairing is the cards adjacent to the end cards, ending with the centre card or pair of cards. The central card or cards give an immediate overview of the outcome.

The Fire String

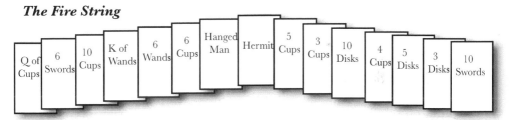

The Hermit as the centre card is the outcome, not generally good for relationships, unless of course we are looking for a secret love affair. Perhaps the people in this String are destined for loneliness together. Alternatively, individual growth is needed before the couple can function well together.

Queen Cups and 10 Swords: Ruin

The 10 Swords is Ruin, so we have a woman who has been hurt, perhaps gone through a break-up or divorce or has had arguments.

6 Swords: Science and 3 Disks: Material Works

She desires to get away or escape or perhaps to learn from what has happened but she has work obligations. Or she is willing to do the work necessary to learn from her experiences or, she hides away in her work.

10 Cups: Perfected Success and 5 Disks: Material Trouble

She is worried about the upsets within the family or being able to support her children financially.

Knight Wands and 4 Cups: Blended Pleasure

Either a man who is bored with life or who cannot slow down to enjoy it.

6 Wands: Victory and 10 Disks: Wealth

He is a successful businessman who has money

6 Cups: Pleasure and 3 Cups: Abundance

He is looking for fun and enjoyment, parties. Or, at some level, he desires the pleasure of a relationship.

Hanged Man and 5 Cups: Loss in Pleasure

But he doesn't know how to go about it and he is thinking about the loss if it went wrong.

Hermit

Either he will remain secretly interested in this woman or he desires a secret love affair. Or at this point he will choose to remain alone.

Summary

Now that we have paired the cards, we can see the bigger picture. It is quite possible that these two people work at the same place. He is the boss and is secretly attracted to her. She has been hurt in a previous relationship and not only is she is not looking for a relationship, but she also wants to escape. Alternatively, they are stuck in a sterile marriage, she wants out and either he does not want this or he is not willing to face the situation. Maybe a single mother trying to support her family; he's been preoccupied with business success but now desires a relationship with her. Afraid of becoming emotionally vulnerable, he has not approached her.

We now have a better picture of who these people are. You do not have to agree with my interpretation and I would hope you have other things to say about this String. As an exercise, try pairing these cards without the book in front of you.

Things to do

Practice on your own String of cards. See if the initial overview matches with the Card Pairings and practice making a story. Do not worry if the story is confused or vague - life is like that! It is also quite possible that the querent does not know the full picture, which is why a tarot reading is required. To keep things simple, I have not distinguished between Major and Minor cards. You may wish to read the Strings in which the Major cards represents events outside the control of the individual and the Minor cards show events that are in the control of the individual.

Pairing from individual Cards

Pairing from individual cards is an easy and quick method for determining the success or failure of a proposed relationship, or how it will develop.

Pairing the cards from opposite ends gives an overview of what is happening in the reading. We do not have to limit ourselves to the extremities – we can pair from either side of any card in the String. As you will see with this method, the court cards see and act in their own way rather than being influenced or changing direction as with Card Counting. In many respects Card Pairing is easier than Card counting – there will always be an equal number of pairs for each String irrespective of where we start, so it is easy to work out the final card or cards. Armed with this knowledge we can make a quick judgement as to outcome. In the tricky question of whether a relationship will work, we can see if the final cards terminate on another court card that the querent will like and then make a more detailed analysis.

To summarise, there are three main methods of card pairing:
* Pairing from the ends to the middle
* Pairing from the Significator
* Pairing from court cards or any other cards

The reader may find that one particular method will work better than the others.

Two obvious candidates for pairing are the Queen of Cups and Knight of Wands but they just do not seem to get together properly.

Pairing from the Queen of Cups

10 Swords: Ruin and 6 Swords: Science

The Queen wants to escape from or understand why she is suffering in career or intellectual pursuits.

3 Disks: Work and 10 Cups: Satiety

Either she wants work in a family atmosphere that is happy or she is prepared to work to create a happy family.

5 Disks: Worry and Knight Wands

The man is broke.

4 Cups: Luxury and 6 Wands: Victory

Conflicting feelings. Perhaps he thinks he has 'won' and doesn't need to do anything or he is dreaming of better times.

10 Disks: Wealth and 6 Cups: Pleasure

He spends his money on luxuries or desires abundance in his life, financially and in relationships.

3 Cups: Abundance and Hanged Man

He likes to suffer, the abundance is delayed for some reason.

5 Cups: Disappointment and Hermit

She thinks she will be on her own or he thinks he will be on his own. Either way, they do not seem capable of facing up to situations. Alternatively, his goals are not likely to be realised and he will be alone.

Pairing from the Knight of Wands

10 Cups: Satiety and 6 Wands: Victory

Since the Knight is a Fire card, he will gravitate to the other fire card, 6 Wands rather than the watery 10 Cups, which is rather aggressive. He probably thinks he is good at family matters. There is conflict between desire for business success and personal life.

6 Swords: Science and 6 Cups: Pleasure

He feels the solution is a holiday away from everything.

Queen Cups and Hanged Man

He sees her as passive, perhaps enjoying suffering. He sees himself as positive and dynamic.

10 Swords: Ruin and Hermit

One or both of them secretly desires to be alone or break up.

5 Cups: Disappointment and 3 Disks: Work

He uses work as an escape, or finds work depressing.

3 Cups: Abundance and 5 Disks: Worry

This is almost a mirror image of the previous pair. He expects things not to improve.

10 Disks: Wealth and 4 Cups: Luxury

The last two pairs show that the man does not feel as wealthy as we thought. The 4 Cups shows he is daydreaming of a better life.

Looking at Reversals with Pairing

Reversed cards fulfil a different function in addition to the one commonly assigned in Tarot. Here we are will used Reversed cards as a means of highlighting groupings, rather than indicating reversed meanings. Where there is obviously a dialogue between two people we can separate out the pairing to show how the actions change.

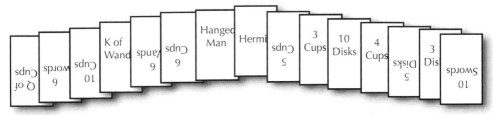

The two court cards in this string are reversed to each other, so we can see the reversed cards as pertaining more to the Queen of Cups, while the other cards are for Knight of Wands. I have slightly rewritten the commentary below so that reversed cards are associated with actions of the Queen Cups, while the other cards are for the Knight Wands.

Queen Cups (reversed) and 10 Swords (reversed)

A woman who has had to face disuption or breakups in her life.

6 Swords (reversed) and 3 Disks

She desires to get away or escape, or perhaps try to learn from what has happened, but she has work obligations.

10 Cups(reversed) and 5 Disks (reversed)

She is worried about being able to support her children financially.

Knight Wands and 4 Cups

A man who is bored with life or can't slow down to enjoy it.

6 Wands (reversed) and 10 Disks

She wants to succeed with this man who she perceives as wealthy.

6 Cups (reversed) and 3 Cups

She is looking for emotional security and happiness, while he just wants fun.

Hanged Man and 5 Cups (reversed)

But he doesn't know how to go about it, and he is thinking about the loss if it went wrong.

Hermit

Either he will remain secretly interested in this woman, or he desires a secret love affair. Or at this point he will choose to remain alone. Since the Hermit is associated with the man, it shows that it is up to him.

Summary

Now that we have paired the cards, we can see the bigger picture. It is quite possible that these two people work at the same place. He is the boss and he is secretly attracted to her but, because she has been hurt in a previous relationship, she is not looking for a relationship and she wants to escape. Maybe she is a single mother trying to support her family, and he's been preoccupied with business success, but now desires a relationship with her. Afraid of becoming emotionally vulnerable, he has not approached her. The emotional hurts are with the woman, but his fear of commitment shows that he would have been hurt in the past, even though he cannot admit it. You do not have to agree with my interpretation, and I would hope you can say other things about this string. As an exercise, try pairing these cards without the book in front of you.

Pairing and Polarity

The Pairing Technique is based upon principles of polarity derived from an understanding of the Tree of Life. Dion Fortune, a Golden Dawn Adept, wrote extensively on the subject. The Three Pillars of the Tree of Life; the Pillar of Severity to the left, the Middle Pillar, and the Pillar of Mercy to the right, are the key to understanding. The Middle Pillar represents the balancing of the two outer forces.

Nothing remains stationary in life so, if the polarity of forces is balanced, at some point energy will start to flow and disequlibrium will start again. Equally, if there is imbalance, forces will commence to regain harmony.

> *Two opposing forces will neutralize each other with a third force, the basis of the Hegelian Dialectic. "Thus the tendency to overflow and the tendency to stabilise form a pair of opposites whose respective influences will always be with us, their relative proportions requiring to be assessed in every given case."*
> Dion Fortune, *Principles of Hermetic Philosophy*

Dion Fortune goes on to say

> *"Polarity… means that everything that exists has two kinds of relationship with any given unit of the non-self at any given moment – it may be of greater energy or lesser energy than the vis á vis; under consideration."*

So, the part with more energy will flow to the part with less energy, and the part with less energy will be in a latent state. Fortune then discusses the Hegelian Dialectic, the basis of Elemental Dignities:

> *"If the force thus sent is in tune with the nature of its vis á vis, that entity will be stimulated into activity and its latent force rendered potent by the breaking up of the equilibriums within its own being and the releasing of the stored energies locked up in them. If the energy sent forth by the more active of the related pair be antipathetic to its vis á vis, it will be resisted and thrown back upon its emanator, producing, not a creative, but a disruptive unbalance, for nothing has been added to its potential resources, they have simply been disarranged."*
> Dion Fortune, *Principles of Hermetic Philosophy*

A stable unit that has equilibrium is inert, and it can only be stimulated into action by another influence. Inertia stores energy, but it is also a bar to progress.

Dion Fortune describes the transition from one plane to another in similar terms:

> *"In order that any thing or factor shall be brought down from a higher to a lower plane, it is necessary to analyse it into the contradictory factors that are held in equilibrium in its nature. To do this, one imagines the opposite extremes of which it is capable and expresses them separately while retaining in consciousness their essential unity when in equilibrium. Equally, if it is desired to raise any factor from a lower to a higher plane, once conceives its opposite and reconciles the pair in imagination and realisation."*
> Dion Fortune, *The Circuit of Force*

The casual reader of Dion's writings will have problems imagining just what those contradictory and extreme factors could be in any situation, but for those of us who routinely pair cards, the Tarot does the work for us! The next paragraph can be seen as a description of the interaction of energies within the Tarot:

> *"Any pair of factors, divided for the sake of manifestation, act and re-act upon each other, alternately struggling to unite and, in the act of re-uniting, exchanging magnetism, and then, their magnetism have been exchanged, repelling each other and striving to draw apart, thus re-establishing their separate individuality; then, this established and a fresh charge of magnetism having been generated, once again they yearn towards each other in order to exchange the charge. It must never be forgotten in this respect that relative potency is not a fixed thing, depending on mechanism or form, but a variable thing, depending on voltage or vitality. Moreover, the charges passes backwards and forwards as an alternating current, never with a permanent one-way flow."*
> Dion Fortune, *The Circuit of Force*

With practice of Pairing and Counting, these forces are a tangible experience. Dion Fortune is describing the mechanics of the magical art as a process of transformation from one plane to another, and with the Opening of the Key Spread, we can see this from the microcosm as the interaction of individual cards that are summed up in each String, and from the macrocosm as the interaction of the Fire and Water Strings to create the third force of the Air or Earth String. Modern writers on Magic, such as Donald Michael Kraig, continually emphasise the importance of performing a Tarot reading in order to divine the consequences of a magical operation. With the Opening of the Key Spread, not only are we given the outcome, but the mechanics of how the energies will work in the ritual (the precise nature of the ritual will of course depend on the knowledge and capabilities of the magician).

The Pairing and Counting Techniques using Elemental Dignities mirrors powerful magical techniques that can be related to the Tree of Life. When we Pair and Count, we are not passive observers in the process, we are actually *creating* that situation in our minds. The process of manifestation proceeds from Unity to the Many and back again. When we start Pairing from the outside, the cards in between can be seen as the product of the Polarities, which gradually decrease to the final card or cards, while when we Pair from an individual card we are proceeding from unity to the greatest number of cards which then decreases to the final card or cards. This can be summed up as:

From Unity to Diversity to Unity

The Caduceus can be seen as symbolising the process of duality, and it is significant that in the Book of Thoth Crowley says:

> *"The importance of this symbol is mainly that the Tarot is primarily the Book of Thoth or Tahuti, the Egyptian Mercury. For the understanding of this book it is necessary to learn how to transmute instinctively and automatically every simple symbol into every complex symbol and back again; for only so is it possible to realize the unity and diversity which is the solution of the cosmic problem."*
> Aleister Crowley, The Book of Thoth

Sephiroth

The Sephiroth can be paired, showing the balance of forces. Chesed, Form, balances the Force of Geburah, so if the Minor Five cards are unbalanced, we should look to the Minor Fours to see if they can be strengthened or have some influence on the situation. Similarly, for Netzach, Emotion, and Hod, Intellect, there needs to be balance. In terms of Tarot, the Eights should balance the Sevens.

Tipareth can be seen as the mediating force or apex of a triangle connecting Chesed/Geburah and Netzach/Hod respectively. The divinatory meanings of the Sixes are almost always positive, which cannot be said for the Fives, Sevens and Eights, and to a lesser extent the Fours.

On the Tree of Life, polarity is relative. For the Pillar of Mercy, Chokmah is positive, Chesed is negative, and Netzach is positive, while in the Pillar of Severity, Binah is negative, Geburah is positive, and Hod is negative. For the central Pillar, Kether is positive, Daath is negative, Tipareth is positive, Yesod is negative, and Malkuth is positive, but this can be reversed depending on the cycle operating.

As in all things, balance is paramount. With Card Pairing a similar process takes place – a pair of cards can be positive to the previous cards, negative to the next pair of cards, or appear neutral. Working with Card Pairing helps us to understand the energies of the Tree of Life for the Querent *at that moment*. Polarity is a fundamental magical concept, so the knowledge gained would be useful for the construction of a magical ritual if required, or if the reading was for information concerning the outcome of a magical ritual. Remember that *any* action performed with intent can be seen as a magical event, so we can advise the querent accordingly how to act. Pairing of course will often throw up information concerning the actions of others, so action advised in accordance with the principles of polarity will be powerful, and requires discretion.

With Card Counting, the card counted is the reconciler between the forces of the cards either side of it, while with Card Pairing, we have the two forces of the paired cards, and we have to reconcile those forces in our own minds as representing events within the situation of the querent. When we Pair cards, we see the subtle stops and flows of energy as we proceed from the outer to the inner – in fact we are following steps that take us from the two outer cards to the central card or cards of the String. There is nothing to stop us starting from the central card and pairing outwards to the outer cards, and so we can extend the concept to pair with any card in the String. Each card is then connected to the others by a matrix of invisible Strings – change the energy or influence of one card, and the effect will spiral out to all the other cards.

Pairing from individual cards is not a requirement, but in some circumstances, particularly where the counting is complex, it is the best way to understand the function of a card in the String. This is particularly useful with the Court cards, as it is only through the cards surrounding a court card that we can see what it represents.

The Stage

Since by definition Pairing will cover all the cards, Card Pairing from the Outer to the Inner represents a stage for the entire cast of characters, so we can see at any particular moment where everyone is in relation to everyone else. Card Pairing from individual cards shows how that actor will relate to all the other cards.

CHAPTER FOUR

The Empress, The Moon and the Fours

III The Empress = 4. Daleth
Water, Venus, Double Letter

XVIII The Moon = 100, Qoph
Water, Pisces, Single Letter

The Empress is on the path that unites Chokmah and Binah, and the Moon card connects Malkuth to Netzach. While the Empress represents the qualities of Venus, fertility and beauty, the Moon has negative connotations. Interestingly, the image of the Dark Towers and the winding path could be taken to be an image of what might be seen on the Path of the Empress as she faces towards Kether. Chesed as number four is the Sephirah of stability, order and reliability, ruled by Jupiter. The numeration of the Empress and Moon is 104; AB HMVN means, "Father of the mob or multitude", DQ is "crushed, fine or thin, dust", Midian, MLK DVD, King David, NCHVM, Nahum, SDM, Sodom. One interesting polarity is SGVLH, personal belongings, and SVLCh, giving up, presenting, remitting – in other words the pair represent giving and taking. One last combination is TzDy, or fish hook, the 18th letter, relating to the Emperor.

The High Priestess represents the highest qualities of the Moon, while the other end of the scale is the Moon card, and here it is paired with the Empress. The Priestess is a glyph of light, of potentiality, but she is still a virgin, the Empress has given birth, and we know from the Bible that the verb to know is the euphemism for sexual relations.

To reach Chesed, we move from the Pillar of Severity, across the central path of the High Priestess and Daath, knowledge, to the Path of Mercy. The Empress represents the famous quotation from the Book of the Law, "Love is the Law (Magus), love under Will (The Fool)". The Abyss destroys all notions of Self and possessions – if there is anything of these qualities present, the Adept attempting to cross the Abyss could be destroyed, crushed to dust. Nahum is a minor prophet who foretells the destruction of Ninevah, and his name means "compassion" or "comfort". God commands Jonah to go to Ninevah, but he refuses.

The letter Daleth means a door, and it refers to the planet Venus. Doors control access to other rooms. The Golden Dawn and Alistair Crowley show how the symbol of Venus, the circle atop a cross, can encompass all the Sephiroth on the Tree of Life. The symbolism of the circle and cross parallels the Rose and Cross discussed in the Sun card, which is paired with the High Priestess. Note how the polarity is switched, while the Priestess represents potentiality, the Empress represents manifestation or birth. Isis is again represented, but now she is the mother. In the Empress we have the secret rose, while for the Sun it is entirely explicit. The Empress harmonises and balances Chokmah and Binah, so what little opposition is necessary is symbolised by the 'revolving moons' – quite why there should be two is not made clear.

Crowley suggests the Moon card be called "The Gateway of Resurrection", so while the Empress shows birth, the Moon has rebirth and the threshold of death. In the sequence of Priestess, Empress and the Moon, we have the three phases of Virgin, Mother and Crone. The Sephiroth of Chokmah and Binah have now become "black towers of nameless mystery, of horror and of fear". Instead of the High Priestess, symbol of light who can cross the Abyss we now have Anubis, who stands upon the threshold. There is no light, only darkness, so sight cannot be used here.

The Fours

The magical image of Chesed is a mighty crowned and throned king, a symbol of rule of law. The four sides of a square represent solidity and reliability, a welcome change from the flux and change we have experienced. The crown refers to Kether, while the Throne is associated with Binah, from where we have come from across the Abyss.

4 Wands, Lord of Completion

This card represents the highest idea that can be understood by the intellect, and it is translated into Law, Order and Government, whose establishment cannot be completed without tact and gentleness. The warning is against using more force to impose order since it will rebound and result in the Strife expressed in the 5 Wands.

4 Cups, Lord of Luxury

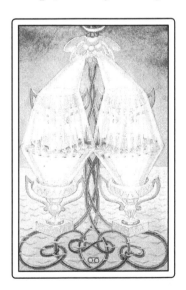

Water does not have the integrity of Fire, so there is instability. Imposing law and order on liquid is a futile exercise, producing the weakness shown in the card.

4 Swords, Lord of Truce

For Crowley, this card symbolizes the idea of militia in their barracks since they are not required until trouble breaks out. At the intellectual level since no opposition is experienced, ideas become dogma.

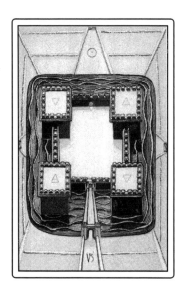

4 Disks, Lord of Power

Power dominates and stabilizes everything. Crowley suggests it represents Law and the Constitution, the Jupiterian influence rather than the element Air with which it is normally associated. The continual movement of the Three Gunas has become the slow turning of squares.

Elemental Dignities

When I first tried to use the Opening of the Key Spread, I fell at the first hurdle. I could not analyse that long string of cards using the normal methods. Over the years of reading and re-reading the Golden Dawn book had taught me that the answers to most questions are in there, but not necessarily in the same chapter. Eventually, I found the answers, and it was simple – analysis starts with the relationship of the elements using the simple rules presented below.

The simplest solution is to look at the elemental relationship between two cards, but I quickly realised that the job was easier if three cards were considered. Instead of the black and white of friends and enemies, subtle shades of grey emerged: a card could be friendly to the card on one side, and an enemy to the card on the other.

The centre card became the Principle, while the cards either side were Modifiers. In this triangle, each card can and does influence the other two for better or worse. This is a classic example of the Dialectic at work: two opposing principles can be resolved through the introduction of a third principle. In this case, we have the third principle – we are simply seeing how it could have got there from the two Modifiers.

At the highest levels, the Dialectic is used to resolve the relationship between God and Man, a subject too complex to go into here, but has relevance when we consider that the primary purpose of the Opening of the Key Spread was for the Golden Dawn Adept to contact his or her Holy Guardian Angel.

How did the Golden Dawn invent Elemental Dignities?

The Golden Dawn books mention Elemental Dignities only in passing, which indicate that there must have been some oral teaching. Perhaps there is a Flying Roll somewhere out there, but for now we have to look for circumstantial evidence.

The rules of ED's are congruent with the basic rules of astrology, but a discussion here is beyond the scope of this book. Of greater interest is the fact that the Golden Dawn advocated the use of the Dialectic in divination. The Divination ritual from the Magical Formulae of the Neophyte Grade is fascinating since it clearly shows that a great amount of thought had gone into divination.

After the spiritual forces had been invoked and the question has been formulated, the diviner is required to formulate arguments for and against success in the object of divination, and to come up with a preliminary judgment. The spiritual forces are again invoked and the formulation of a second judgment is required based upon the development of the first judgment. Then, the two judgments are compared

> *"... so as to enable the Diviner to form an idea of the probable action of forces beyond the actual plane, by the invocation of an angelic figure consonant to the process"*
> Israel Regardie, The Golden Dawn

This process is repeated several times before a final judgment is delivered to the Querent! Not only that, but this process results in a situation where:

> *"The Diviner formulates clearly with what forces it may be necessary to work in order to combat the Evil, or fix the Good, promised by the divination."*
> Israel Regardie, The Golden Dawn

The Golden Dawn does not define the method of divination, so it could be the tarot or other methods. However, there is a precedent for this method in Geomancy, where the manipulation of the geomantic figures results in the creation of Left Witness and Right Witness from which the Judge figure is created. There is another step whereby the Reconciler is created.

The description of the divination ritual above shows that the Tarot cards need to be anchored to something, and rather than maintain the relative positions of the sequence of cards, another method of understanding the relationships between each group of three cards is to see them as Supernal Triangles.

The Supernal Triangle & the Four Elements

The use of the Supernal Triangle helps in understanding the invisible forces that define the nature of those three cards so that they can be seen as acting as one unit. In other words, the influence of the Supernal Triangle is to unify the three cards. The consequences of the actions within the Supernal Triangle are manifested further down the Tree of Life, so in a Tarot reading this manifestation would be the events that have either happened or may happen in the future.

It is the art of the Diviner to discern the subtle flows of energy between these Supernal Triangles so that he or she can advise the Querent wisely. Since the Supernal Triangle is the origin of actions, Magicians can influence the events represented by the use of Will, for better or worse.

We attribute qualities to the Triangle, such as God, the Father, and the Son in Christianity. Shiva, Vishnu and Brahma in Vedic philosophy represent the concept of Destruction, Maintenance and Creation, which appears as the Three Gunas. Of the Fortune Card in the Thoth Tarot deck, (which has a Triangle at the centre of the wheel), Aleister Crowley says:

> "In the Hindu system are three Gunas – Sattvas, Rajas and Tamas. The word "Guna" is untranslatable. It is not quite an element, a quality, a form of energy, a phase, or a potential; all these ideas enter into it. All the qualities that can be predicated of anything may be ascribed to one or more of these Gunas: Tamas is darkness, inertia, sloth, ignorance, death and the like; Rajas is energy, excitement, fire, brilliance, restlessness; Sattvas is calm, intelligence, lucidity and balance."
> Aleister Crowley, Book of Thoth

In Astrology the Triangle manifests as the Triplicity of Cardinal, Fixed and Mutable qualities of the signs of the Zodiac. The Trine aspect of 120 degrees connects each element through the Triplicity. Alchemically, we have the three Principles of Nature: Salt, Sulphur and Mercury. The Triangle unites these concepts, but that still does not tell us anything about the Triangle itself.

From early times, the Triangle has been used as a symbol for the four elements. The upward pointing triangles represent action, while the downward triangles show passivity. The horizontal line through the Air and Earth triangles shows that they are derived from the primary elements of Fire and Water.

The Triangle is the basis of the Tree of Life. In fact, there are three Triangles, with the topmost known as the Supernal Triangle. The first point of the Supernal Triangle is known as Kether or Crown. A crown is something that is lowered onto the head. Beyond or before Kether is another Trinity:

AYN: Negative
AYN SVP: Limitless
AYN SVP AVR: Limitless Light

Note that again we have a trinity – each word has three letters. From Kether emanates a line to the next sephirah of Chokmah, Wisdom. The second line from Kether goes to Binah, Knowledge.

Conceptually, there is very little difference between these positions. It is only further down the Tree that difference becomes manifest. Philosophically, the Tree of Life is the manifestation of Something from Nothing (AYN). The interplay of opposites is crucial here, and is known as the Hegelian Dialectic of Thesis, Antithesis and Synthesis. The polarity of Positive and Negative is resolved in Synthesis, but in the Supernal Triangle, Synthesis emanates Thesis and Antithesis. It is only beyond Daath, the Eleventh Sephirah that difference is manifest. The significance of the Supernal Triangle and Magick is developed in Chapter 6.

Elemental Dignity Rules

Each card is assigned an element based on the following pattern:

A Major Arcana's element is based on its Elemental, Planetary or Zodiac attribution. See the card descriptions at the beginning of each chapter for details.

The Minor Arcana's elements are:

Wands = Fire
Cups = Water
Swords = Air
Disks = Earth

The Four Elements interact with each other using rigid rules:
•   Fire and Water are enemies, therefore weaken each other
•   Air and Earth are enemies, therefore weaken each other
All other combinations are friendly, therefore strengthen each other.
•   Fire and Air are active
•   Water and Earth are passive.

The System

Tarot cards can be read easily using the Four Elements as a basis, to determine quickly and simply the most important cards, their strengths and weaknesses, and how they interact with each other to gain information that may have been apparent only through intuition. The steps for analyzing any group of three cards can be summarized as:

- Strongest card
- Weakest card
- Excess of an element
- Influence of a 'missing' element
- Is the Principal card active or passive?
- Major/Minor/Court
- Dignity
- Reversed cards

Once you have done this, actually apply and combine the meanings of each card with appropriate weighting. This is such an important point - the meaning of the individual cards is the last thing you look at! If this sounds strange advice, in some respects we deal with situations in our daily life in similar ways. When we walk into a room full of strangers, we instinctively know how to act simply by observing the position, actions and attitudes of the people. We know when to be deferential, arrogant, polite, friendly, stand-offish, cold, good humoured, and intimidating. These attitudes change as we work our way across groups of people in the same room, meeting friends, strangers, enemies, colleagues and family members.

Before we interpret the Fire Sequence, here are examples of interpreting permutations of three different elements in the three positions.

Fire, Air and Water

Earth provides stability and support to Fire and Water, but is an enemy of Air. In each of the three situations below, we should expect a lack of practicality, or situations that cannot last.

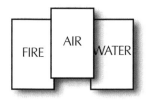

The centre card Air is friendly with Fire and Water, so it is strengthened. It is active, therefore whatever it represents is likely to happen. Note that Fire and Water are enemies, so that the Principal card is even stronger, and can rise over any problems caused by the modifiers. Fire actively supports Air, while Water provides a passive, more emotional role. We could be looking at a thought or idea that is trying to reconcile conflicting actions and feelings. The lack of Earth suggests abstract thought, or theoretical ideas that would not work in a practical situation.

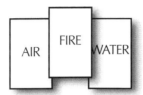

Fire is friendly with Air but weakened by Water. Air is the strongest card. However, the Modifiers are friendly to each other and are therefore stronger. As Fire is active, and Air supports, the event is likely to happen, but not without either emotional turmoil or a complete disregard for feelings. This could be an action that attempts to be rational and logical, but founders for lack of emotional support. The absence of Earth prevents any action from having a solid, long-lasting basis.

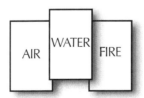

The Principal is passive, while the modifiers are active. Fire is inimical to the Principal and weakens it, while Air strengthens. The Modifiers are friendly. The conclusion is that we have an unsatisfactory situation that is unlikely to change quickly. The Principal is likely to be pulled in different directions. This combination is the weakest we have seen so far. Water is extremely uncomfortable - it is being stirred up or channelled in directions that it does not want to go. Water requires support - it needs a container, and the lack of Earth highlights the volatility of the situation. The Water could be imagined as steam or a cloud in the air.

Fire, Water and Earth

Air is missing, so there will be a lack of intellect, discrimination, and thought. The potential for conflict is lessened, particularly as there are now two passive elements and one active. Since Fire and Water are enemies, we would expect Earth to be stronger in any position.

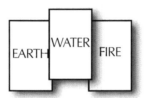

Water is the Principal card; it is supported by Earth, but weakened by Fire. We have a basically settled situation that gets concentrated with time - the Earth thickens the Water, while the Fire turns the heat up. The modifiers are friendly to each other, and they could be seen to gang up on Water, which is under great pressure. Since Air is missing, perhaps a better method would be to apply persuasion and reasoned thought.

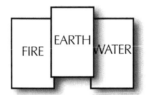

Earth is the strongest since it is between the fighting elements of Fire and Water. It is as though it is dividing and ruling simply by being there. Earth wins by endurance - it soaks up the Water, and the Fire heats up the Water to steam, unless of course the Water does not douse the flames. I see an image of a lit candle. Since Earth is so strong, the lack of Air is even weaker.

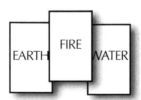

Once again Earth wins. Fire is the Principal, but it is weakened by Water, and since Earth and Water are friends, the heat could be extinguished. If the situation is more benign, we see the Earth and Water combining as a fuel, supporting the actions of Fire. There is no finesse, only brute force without the influence of Air, but on the other hand, Fire does need oxygen to continue burning.

Fire, Air and Earth

Obviously Water is missing, so we know that this combination will be predominantly active, Earth will be weakest since it is an enemy of Air, and Fire will in general be strongest as it is friendly with Air. The lack of Water will indicate absence of compassion, comfort, and any emotional content.

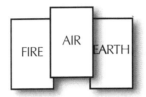

The modifiers are friendly to each other, providing a solid base for the thoughts represented by Air. Unfortunately Earth acts like a dead weight, while Fire urges action on Air. The thinking process will be utilitarian and functional, possibly brutal, and any actions contemplated will be done without consideration of the feelings and needs of other. Water is desperately needed as a lubricant.

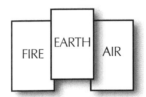

Earth is very weak - it is being urged into action by Fire and Air, which is a quality alien to it. In fact, one could see the Earth as literally 'putting a lid' on any action. When Earth gives way, the backpressure released could be explosive. Thinking laterally, Earth as the basis shows it being left behind by the rapid ascent of Fire and Air. Such an action would probably not last for long. Again, Water is necessary to act as a lubricant in the first case, or possibly as fuel in the second.

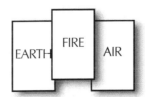

Fire is very strong: it has material basis (Earth), and intelligent control (Air). The only problem is that I hope the actions contemplated show some kind of compassion and consideration. Without Water I very much doubt it. These are qualities of Establishment and Action, quite possibly of the police or military. Processes started that are difficult to stop.

Water, Air and Earth

Two passive elements, and Air and Earth are enemies. The simple conclusion is that Air will be the weakest element. We have a kind of daydreaming scenario - certainly without fire there will be little action.

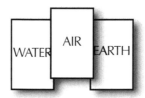

The intellect and analytical skills are the focus, but there is little to inspire. If the imagination is fertile (Earth and Water are fecund), we could expect inspiration, but the mind here is feeble and unable to cope - nothing can be done without Fire. We have an image of bubbles rising up through a swamp. Fire would be the catalyser, converting the chemical processes into heat. Certainly the introduction of a spark into the foetid gases would be explosive.

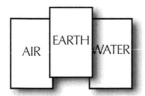

Another mixed situation where the modifiers are friendly to each other, but Air and Earth are enemies. One could see this situation as fog over the ground. Air is fairly weak, and without the energy of Fire, not a lot will happen to clear the atmosphere.

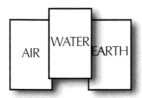

Bubbles and detritus suspended in the water. One could also see fishes and plant life in a pond or lake, perhaps by the seashore. No fire to warm up the situation. There is the fertility of the Arctic and Antarctic oceans. Water is very comfortable here, surrounded by friends.

Analysis of the Fire String by Elemental Dignity

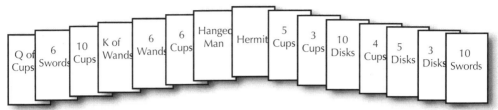

We will start with the 10 Swords, which is the top card. Since we read Elemental Dignities in groups of three, we include the bottom card, the Queen of Cups, since the String can be seen as a circle.

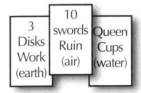

The centre or Significator card is considered to be one of the worst tarot cards! Fortunately it is not the strongest card, which is the Queen, since she is friendly with both Air and Earth, while the 3 Disks and 10 Swords weaken each other. Looked at in this light, we have to moderate the influence of 10S to something like "The woman wants to make a new start by breaking away from an unhappy situation". The combination of cards is more passive than active, and of course we need the influence of Fire to get things going. Notice that there are only two fire cards in the entire String, so we would not expect major changes at once, particularly since as we will see, they are to do with the man involved! There is a preponderance of Minor cards in this String, so efforts are down to the individual.

Working left from the 10 Swords we have:

Earth and Air are enemies, so the earth cards are strongest, but an excess of an element is not necessarily good. It is as if the 10 Swords is trying to divide and unsettle the two Earth cards.. This is not a happy combination – the expectations of success in anything are very low. If we assume the cards are to do with the woman, it would seem she has been hurt before, and she thinks more of the same will happen again. There is no emotional feeling (water) and she is uncertain as to what to do (no fire). She is probably agitated (mental frustration caused by lack of fire to spur progress). The effect of the two earth cards is to slow progress.

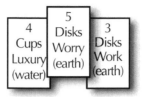

The 4 Cups is friendly with the other two earth cards, and all of them are passive.

At last we have some feelings, but the 4 Cups usually feels pretty flat. It shows boredom, no excitement. Maybe that is what she is feeling about life. The Significator, 5 Disks is not a happy card, so again low expectations probably arising from negative experiences from the past.

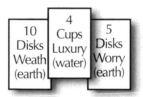

This permutation is similar to the previous three, but now the Water card is the Significator. The picture is of a lake or puddle of water, surrounded by land. Maybe someone has offered a carrot in the form of a job elsewhere, or the Querent desires more money, or she is looking at the company pension: the tens show change, so her feelings about security are what have to change.

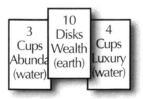

Two Water cards surrounding an Earth card show a passive, friendly influence, but now there is excess water, so the emotions are coming to the fore. The Querent is probably dreaming of what she would do with that money – new clothes, parties, celebrations, going out for a drink, anything to get her out of her dreary situation.

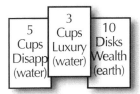

Since the 10 Swords, we have had combinations of only earth and water. This combination is a variation of the cards around the 4 Cups. Here optimism remains fragile – her reverie is brought down to earth by the feelings of failure emanating from the 5 cups. She is looking down the road, and sees that the happiness promised by the 3 cups is transitory.

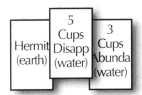

A Major card, one of the only two in this String, but we still have 2 water and one earth. Positively, we could see her looking inwards for answers, or perhaps making steps to go on a self-development course. Since it is a major card, perhaps she saw an advert. Alternatively, something happened to make her think she will remain lonely in her life. Even though we have the joyful 3 cups, the String shows that they remain dreams.

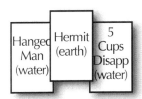

This is a picture of isolation from emotions and feelings. Now the Querent doesn't know what to do at all. The feeling of stagnancy and loss is rather pervasive. Something happens to make her feel this.

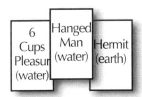

At last a more positive card, but we still have this combination of earth and water. It is as if the Querent wishes to enjoy herself, but she is fearful that as soon as she does have fun and pleasure there will be sacrifice and loss.

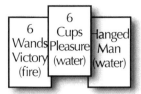

The fire card is very weak since the watery cards are enemies and will try to swamp it. However, the inclusion of fire results in the 6 Cups Pleasure, whereas in the previous three cards, the outcome resulted in the loss of the Hanged Man.

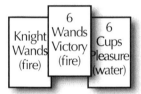

Now we have all positive cards, but the pleasure of the 6 cups is getting squeezed. In the previous examples where we looked at the General Picture, the Card Pairing and Card Counting, it was clear that this is the man that she wanted to get away from, and he was portrayed as something of the devil, but perhaps it is her own perception that colours the picture. Alternatively, he can be seen as an overwhelmingly positive man who comes into her life. By now you are probably thinking she needs to get out more – she needs fun and excitement, and he could supply it. The Fire and Water conflicts, but Fire is getting stronger, so change is more likely.

Perhaps he is the same man. The 10 cups is a very positive card, but next to the fire of the other two cards there is discomfort. Note that because there are only 2 fire cards, and they are surrounded by water, we know nothing can ever get going, so perhaps there is a part of her that prefers to stay the same way, despite two active cards. If we take this triplet on its merits, divorced from the previous cards, we would say that this is a dynamic successful man whose home life is pretty good, but he does not stay in much, or does not appreciate the stability he gets from home.

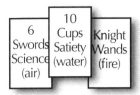

Finally we have a combination that has three elements. The 6 swords is strongest because it is friendly with fire and water, who are inimical to each other. Two active cards make for a more dynamic situation. If they are a couple, perhaps he is suggesting a second honeymoon.

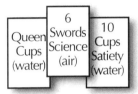

Two water and air are friendly, but still predominantly passive. In the previous triplet, it looked like the Knight wanted to escape, and here we have a similar situation, but she is less likely to act.

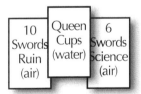

The 10 Swords takes us back to the beginning of the String. A passive woman surrounded by uncomfortable thoughts about taking action. She wants to change and improve her life but she fears the consequences. These are friendly cards and mostly active, so she is likely to do something about it, at least actively confront her problem and search for a solution.

This is a good point to remind us of the cards surrounding the Knight.

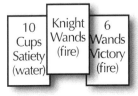

His fire is going to disrupt her passive Water. There is a powerful sexual alchemy of fire and water at work. Perhaps his sexuality was the main attraction to her at the beginning, and she is wondering were it has gone. Since Fire and Air have an affinity through action, he is certainly the catalyst. In total we have two fire cards, two water cards and two air cards involved in and around them – no earth to bring the situation down to practicalities. The actions of the man make the woman think, but she doesn't seem capable of making changes to her life.

Elemental Dignities and Spirit

For those of you who are comfortable with using Elemental Dignities and feel the need to be stretched, here is one way the system can be developed. The truth is, there may well be five categories of Tarot not four. The Golden Dawn hints at such but does not give details.

When we read Tarot using Elemental Dignities, the four elements are a fundamental aspect of the teaching. Each card interacts equally with each other, but the **outcome** for an individual card can be stronger or weaker, more active, or less passive, depending on the surrounding cards. When we deal with the energy levels of a greater number of cards, we see a hierarchy of dignity developing.

Having worked with Elemental Dignities for years, I have noticed certain anomalies, but it has taken time to clarify the rules, which might explain them. The study of Elemental Dignities is the study of the transformation of energy through the four elements. The Rules are clear, but it appears that some of the cards hint at greater and profound transformations happening within the reading, which give the Reader clues as to how to advise on spiritual transformation for the Querent.

Kabbalistic knowledge and the teaching of Tarot give us clues that this interaction is not as rigid as the rules of Elemental Dignities suggest. To begin, here are the cards that are in the class of Spirit or Akasha:

Tarot	Category	Tree of Life
Fool		
Magus		
High Priestess	Major	Supernal
Four Aces		Kether
	Minor	
Four Tens		
Four Princesses	Court	Malkuth

Each category of the Tarot is represented in roughly the correct proportions - three Major cards, eight Minor cards and four Court cards. All the cards are associated with either Kether or Malkuth, and as we know, 'Malkuth is Kether, but after another way'. Since I doubt you have seen such a category before, here is some internal evidence from the Golden Dawn, Tarot and Kabbalah that it exists.

Major Cards and Kether

The Fool, Magus and High Priestess are associated with Paths on the Tree of Life that originates from Kether, the Crown, which is beyond the four elements. Astrologically, the Magus is associated with Mercury, a planet that does not have an elemental attribution - it takes on the elemental attributes of the sign or house it resides in. The Fool is associated with Uranus, a planet that brings instability and change in whatever region of the horoscope we find it. Likewise, the High Priestess as the Moon brings change and fluctuation.

Air is attributed to the Fool, but it is defined as RVCh, Spirit. Note also that the Fool card is attributed to Air, but when we consider the YHVH attributions, this Atziluthic level is Fire.

The Magus has a slightly different status. Most depictions of the card show the Magus having mastery over the four elements, which is an attribute of Spirit. The balanced appearance of the four elements is a sign of Akasha, known as Osiris in the Golden Dawn Enochian system.

Minor Cards

The Golden Dawn describes the Aces as the 'Roots of the Powers of the Elements':

> *The first in order and appearance are the four Aces, representing the force of the Spirit acting in, and binding together the four scales of each element and answering to the Dominion and Letters of the Name in the Kether of each. They represent the Radical or Root-Force and are said to be placed on the North Pole of the Universe, wherein they revolve, governing its revolution, and ruling as the connecting link between Yetsirah and Assiah.*
> Israel Regardie, The Golden Dawn

This indicates that the Aces are Spirit, not the elements themselves. When considering Elemental Dignities, we need to do the same. Papus describes the Aces as 'commencement of commencement', or in other words, beginning of the beginning. Nothing has actually happened yet.

The Tens are an appendage to the Tree of Life, and in Papus' system have an indeterminate outcome depending on 'the card which follows it'. There is the objection that Malkuth represents Earth, but this is illusory. In Kabbalah, the element Earth does not really exist. The 'Mother Letters' represent Fire, Water and Air - Earth is not represented.

Court Cards

The Princesses have a unique status within the Tarot. Although they are attributed to the four elements, they are part of Malkuth, which as we have seen has indeterminate status, a characteristic of all the cards discussed here. The Princesses are associated with Kether, particularly the Aces. Unlike the Knights, Queen and Princes, the Princesses do not have an astrological attribution. The Golden Dawn defines the powers of the Court cards thus:

* Potential Power is the Knight
* Brooding Power is the Queen
* Power in Action is the Prince
* Reception and Transmission is the Princess

The Princess has an entirely different function to the other court cards. She is there to receive energy and to send it on to the next stage indicated by the Aces and North Pole as shown in the quotation above. It is quite possible that this energy is not necessarily transformed, something else to consider in Elemental Dignities.

Applying Spirit to Elemental Dignities

When analysing any of the above cards in a reading using Elemental Dignities, you may well find that the inimical influence is distinctly moderated. In other words, these cards, even though they have elemental attributions, do not have such harsh effects. Equally, the interpretation of them is dependent on the surrounding cards.

Another way of looking at the Spirit cards is that they show areas where either change is about to happen and the Querent is either unaware of this change, or that they represent areas that the Querent has only vague intimations. Do not get me wrong - apply the rules of friendship and enemies, active and passive equally to all the cards, but do have an awareness of subtleties. The interpretation of individual cards does not change - the prognostication of the 10 Swords is as bad as it always was!

CHAPTER FIVE

The Emperor, The Star and the Fives

IV The Emperor = 90, Tzaddi
Fire, Aries, Single Letter

XVII The Star = 5, Heh
Air, Aquarius, Single Letter

Aleister Crowley famously transposed the Hebrew letters of these two cards, after an instruction in the Book of the Law, and it is interesting that the Pairing would bring these two cards together whether or not they were transposed. The numerical value of the cards is 5 + 90 = 95, which relates to HMN, Venus and MADYM, Mars (planetary ruler of Geburah), HMYM the Waters, MHLK journey, MLKH Queen, and ZBVLN Capricorn.

The Emperor card combines the idea of energy in its most material form with the idea of authority, and the card represents the idea of alchemical Sulphur. The action is sudden and violent, but does not last. Crowley makes it clear that his authority is derived from the Word of the Magus. The Star card, which was transposed by Crowley with the Emperor card, represents Nuith as manifestation of form, as opposed to the force of the Emperor, and the Star of Venus is strongly associated with her, which connects with the Empress.

Depicted within the Star card are the Great Mother, the Great Sea of Binah and the Abyss, so clearly we are still developing ideas from the High Priestess and the Empress cards. Within this card, Crowley polarises the old school of classical physics and the curvature of space in Einstein's theories. Bernhard Riemann (1826 – 1866) developed non-Euclidean geometry – "Riemann saw that a geometry is simply a space with enough extra structure to be able to measure things like lengths." (History of Mathematics, Fauvel and Gray, 1987). Spacetime is curved, and again Crowley introduces the idea of "spiral force".

The Fives

We have crossed from the Pillar of Mercy and Chesed over the Central Pillar to the Pillar of Severity. To break from the settled rather complacent feeling of the Fours to the Fives requires great energy. Fives are difficult numbers, indicating violence, anger and pain, but they are a natural correction, and usually indicate the result of not doing enough. The Fives in Tarot generally suggest corrective motion that has to be applied, which is usually uncomfortable.

The presence of all 4 Fives indicate discipline and order (All elements are present), while three of them show quarrels.

5 Wands, Lord of Strife

At its highest levels, this card represents purgation, the rising of the phoenix, mitigated by the influence from the Mother in Binah. On the card is the wand of the Chief Adept, whose authority comes from on high.

5 Cups, Lord of Disappointment

The energy of fire upsets the placid nature of water, causing lack of ease just when things seemed to be going fine. The anticipated pleasure has been destroyed.

5 Swords, Lord of Defeat

Defeat results from insufficient effort to maintain the armed peace of the 4 Swords, resulting in quarrels. Pacifism or treachery is often to blame.

5 Disks, Lord of Worry

Indicates the breakdown of the economic system – there is no balance between social orders. Crowley includes all four

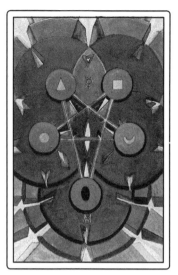

elements and Spirit, or the five Tattvas in this card as holding down some kind of evil organism from a lower plane. In this context, the 5 Disks is one of continued suppression of evil.

Card Counting - The Golden Dawn Tarot Sutras

The word sutra means 'thread' and is an aphoristic style of writing in ancient Vedic and Buddhist texts. Each sutra can be very short – in Sanskrit, the verses of Patanjali's Yoga Sutras are on average only six words long. To compensate, a tradition of Commentary has arisen. We find the same situation in the Sepher Yetsirah, which is incomprehensible without the Commentaries. In line with sacred texts, these works have generally remained unchanged throughout the centuries.

Translator Alistair Shearer says of Sutras:

> *"As the nodes of what was, and still is, essentially an oral teaching, the sutras are almost like lecture notes, mnemonics. Each sutra resembles a knot of the finest thread that must be teased out and unravelled, so that every inch of its meaning is displayed. Only then can the whole fabric of the teaching be woven together."*
> *Alistair Shearer, Effortless Being: the Yoga Sutras of Patanjali*

Anyone who has worked on the Opening of the Key Spread will recognise a similar process to the sutras taking place. The Counting Technique can be seen as following a thread through the reading that unites apparently unconnected cards. The process of unravelling the knots of the reading is a familiar experience too. The other point to this quotation is that just as the sutras can be seen as mnemonics, we only need basic interpretations of the cards in order to make the system work.

Now of course in-depth knowledge of each card is desirable, but the emphasis of so many tarot books and tarot teachers on memorising the meanings of each card is not necessary, and intimidating to new students. The various techniques of card counting, card pairing and elemental dignities when reading the Opening of the Key Spread serve to bring about an in depth picture of the reading. Each technique brings about a different aspect to the reading that can be integrated into the entire picture. Furthermore, the interpretation of each card changes slightly according to the technique used, and the position of the card in the sequence.

Due to the cross-fertilization between the members of the Golden Dawn and the Theosophical Society, Eastern texts were widely disseminated and discussed. Indeed Aleister Crowley translated Eastern texts. The aphoristic style is seen in the I Ching, where we only have the hexagrams of six lines – the imagination of the I Ching Diviner is required to 'see' pictures. Sixty-four hexagrams is not that much different from the 78 tarot cards, so why do we have this emphasis on looking at the pictures of the tarot cards to "discern the meaning". The I Ching has been around for thousands of years, and if pictures were really required, they would have been done a long time ago.

The word Sutra has an exalted status in the east – we have the Yoga Sutras, the Brahma Sutras, the Shiva Sutras, even the Diamond Sutras of Buddhist thought. The weaving of threads into the warp and woof of cloth is a powerful symbol of unity seen in Islam and North American Natives. The string is a powerful symbol in the West. In Physics we have the Superstring Theories that are fundamental to understanding the origin of our Universe. Another string familiar to biologists is the strands of DNA; the sequencing of the four nucleic acids defines our genetic makeup. The Strands of DNA are wound in a helix, and then into a knot found in the nucleus of every living cell. The importance of sequencing the four nucleic acids in DNA parallels the interpretation of Elemental Dignities in the Opening of the Key spread.

DNA Helix

The deck of 78 tarot cards can be seen as a compressed string. After being shuffled and cut, the tarot reader will take the top 5 to perhaps 20 cards and deal them out into various patterns. Now of course, in the light of this discussion, the reader will be asking why not the rest? This is a question I have been asking the tarot community for many years, without a satisfactory answer. Tarot readers are only looking at the visible 1/10th of an iceberg.

An important rule when reading the Opening of the Key spread is **"do not change the order of the cards"**. All other spreads require placing the cards in isolation in positions that are supposed to define love, work, health, past, future, etc. This of course destroys the order of the cards. By working with the Opening of the Key Spread for many years, I have come to realise that although the cards are cut into four piles that are sequenced, in reality we still have one sequence of 78 cards.

The Opening of the Key spread takes that compressed sequence of cards and puts them in four more manageable sequences that can be interpreted by the reader. Now, although all 78 cards are available for reading, experience shows that in practice only a small fraction of the cards are read. In the preceding Lessons and Examples I have analysed the same cards in the same sequence or String exhaustively to illustrate the process. In real life, with experience, the Tarot reader will know which technique is applicable. As you will see, it is the tarot cards themselves that will point out the cards to look at in depth. There are times when I have pondered a string of cards wondering where to start, and the querent will suddenly point to one of the cards, which is usually the same one that I have been considering starting with! Invariably that card is found in the most complex or difficult string of cards, but that is sometimes the lot of the tarot reader!

In this book, a "pile" is a number of cards stacked up, while a "string" is a sequence of cards fanned out for reading. Some of the techniques used are not found in the original Golden Dawn documentation, but they have worth in helping the reader. Since one of the aims of this book is to make the Golden Dawn Tarot Techniques more accessible to the tarot reader, I have also taken the liberty of not following the Golden Dawn system of starting with Card Counting and then Card Pairing.

The patterns revealed in these strings of cards are fascinating, and the implications of how this information can be used to reveal secret or hidden activities, which may not even be known to the Querent, or may indeed to refer to magic whether of the Black or White variety and how to deal with any magical acts, is discussed in the next few chapters.

Introduction to Counting Methods

If you have been working through the previous chapters examples, you should be thoroughly familiar with strings of cards. The next stage is to read the same strings using the Golden Dawn Counting Technique. With the Counting Technique, we start at a card of choice (usually the Court Card representing the querent) and count along the string a certain number of cards, building up a story as we go. For example from an Ace we would count five cards along the string and examine that particular card as the next 'instalment' of an unfolding story.

The Counting Rules are in the next table, and with time they are easily memorised. Remember to include the card you are starting from in the count!

Aces	5 cards (the five elements)
Kings, Queens, Princes	4 cards (the four letters of YHVH)
Princesses	7 cards (the seven palaces of Malkuth)
Minor Cards	2 to 10 cards (same as card number)
Fool, Judgment, Hanged Man	3 cards (the three seed elements)
Zodiac Major Cards	12 cards (the twelve signs of the Zodiac)
Planetary Major Cards	9 cards (the seven planets + the moons nodes)

Direction of Counting

When initially counting from cards upright is clockwise and reversed is counterclockwise. The exception is the Court Cards where the Queen and Princess count clockwise and the Knights and Princes counterclockwise. This is reversed if the card is reversed. When a Court Card is 'hit' the counting changes to their direction. When we 'hit' the same card from the same direction, that is the end of the counting.

Analysing the Fire String using Card Counting

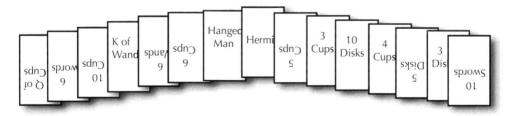

The overview of the Fire String in Chapter One showed the incipient breakdown of a relationship between a man and a woman. The woman in particular seemed very frustrated at the lack of progress. The 10 Swords would be a reasonable place to start from counting, as would the main protagonists, the Queen of Cups and the Knight of Wands.

10 Swords - Anti-clockwise

We start and end with the treachery of the 10 Swords, and note how all the cards are reversed in this counting sequence. The 10 Swords is surrounded by the 3 Disks, an inimical element, and the Queen herself at the other end of the String.

10 Swords, Ruin (reversed) Disruption and disorder surround the situation. Reason and logic divorced from reality. We then count 10 to:

6 Cups, Pleasure (reversed) The contrary feeling of a desire for happiness. The Queen seems to simultaneously desire the relationship to work as much as fail. The Hanged Man next to her supports the feeling of failure. Count 6 to:

Queen Cups (reversed) The Queen has the contrary feelings of divorce (10 Swords) with the desire for escape and learning more about herself and why she finds herself in such predicaments (6 Swords). All three 6's are involved in this sequence, and together they mean 'success and gain', however this success seems somewhat confused. Count 4 to:

5 Disks, Worry (reversed) But her experience of life so far has been negative, which is how she continues to perceive the situation. The cards surrounding, the 4 Cups and 3 Disks, indicate she is bored with work too. Count 5 to:

5 Cups, Disappointment (reversed) And she does not expect it to improve. The Hermit and 3 Cups surrounding show that things are really not that bad! Perhaps she wants to be alone. Count 5 to:

6 Wands, Victory (reversed) She knows that the only way to change her life is to do something about it herself, but notice that the Knight of Wands and 6 Cups are adjacent, which possibly suggests that she feels intimidated by the success she feels the Knight is achieving in his life. Count 6 to:

10 Swords, Ruin (reversed) But she can only see the chaos it will create. Alternatively, because this card follows on from the Knight, ruin and despair is all that she feels. Count ends.

10 Swords – Clockwise

Reversing the count reveals some familar cards, which suggests that the Querent feels that whatever she will do will go wrong.

Counting 10 clockwise, we find ourselves on the 5 cups, Disappointment, which is surrounded by the 3 Cups and the Hermit. One card expresses parties and joy, while the other wants to be alone. It seems as if neither congeniality nor solitude will work, suggesting that either person is depressed. From the 5 Cups we count 5 to the 5 Disks. The Fives always show that the problems are self-inflicted, so she cannot blame anyone else, even if she wants to. As a Tarot Reader, I would put that a bit more diplomatically, but around the 5 Disks are the 4 Cups and 3

Disks. The 4 Cups shows boredom, while the 3 Wands shows the beginning of an action, and the next card is the 10 Swords! Perhaps he tries to initiate a divorce, but she does not want it, condemning both to a living hell.

We count 5 to the 6 Swords, Science, and this card often represents travel. It is adjacent to the Queen of Cups. Is this the woman he sees in his mind, or is she another woman? The counting string tells us the result: we count 6 to the Hanged Man and then 3 to the 5 Cups, Disappointment, which ends the counting. Since it is obvious we are dealing with relationships, the next is naturally to look at the two Court cards in the String.

Queen of Cups Anticlockwise

The Queen is reversed, so we will start by counting in the reversed direction, ie anticlockwise. She is at the bottom of the String, at the far end from the 10 Swords, but since the String can be considered to be joined in a circle, she is adjacent to it, with the 6 Swords on the other side. I usually run through the sequence fairly quickly to get a feel of what is going on. In this direction the Queen is the start and finish of the String, and it includes the 10 Swords just before returning to her. As we will see, even though she is part of the counting sequence for the 10 Swords, the outcome is different.

Queen Cups (reversed) The Queen is between the conflicting feelings of 6 Swords, Science, and 10 Swords, Ruin. Even though Water is friendly with Air, she will be undergoing mental torment. Count 4 to:

5 Disks Worry See 10 Swords above. Earth follows on naturally from Air, so she is looking at what she perceives the outcome to be, which is worries for the future. Count 5 to:

5 Cups Disappointment Then she looks to the past, and sees her life as a waste in many respects. Count 5 to:

6 Wands Victory Tinged with some good moments, but has the sacrifice (Hanged Man) beenworth the achievements (6 Wands)? Count 6 to:

10 Swords Ruin Whatever the merits of the past, for good or bad, it is time to make the break. She cannot console herself with the successes. She has to admit that she is unhappy and move on.

6 Cups Pleasure She seems to enjoy the somewhat similar feeling of failure (6 Wands reversed) with the loss of the Hanged Man. We then return to the Queen of Cups.

Queen Cups Clockwise

This Sequence is very short, a loop between her and the Knight Wands. Since the Queen is reversed, this sequence would not necessarily be considered. Elementally, we would not expect this combination to work. The Knight would be aggressive, good at starting things, impatient, and bored easily, while the Queen Cups is reflective, dreamy, romantic, slow to act, and prefers to agree with others, finding a consensus. The Knight would be constantly agitating her. He would want an adventure holiday, with sports and activities, while she would prefer to read a good book on the beach. It is time to inspect the path taken by the Knight.

Knight Wands Clockwise

There are five cards in the clockwise string, and they have a familiar feel to them – they are part of the Queen's count, and the 10 Swords. If we needed proof that these people are connected, this is it.

On the face of it, we have positive cards, but of course Water and Fire are inimical. The 6 Wands shows his winning, aggressive 'can do' attitude, while the 10 Cups is of course passive. He is probably telling people that his marriage is fine, and she is happy!

Hanged Man Where did all that positive energy go? He must be telling himself he is successful and dynamic, otherwise he might forget! The surrounding cards, 6 Cups and Hermit, show that actually he is a private man, who prefers time on his own. Perhaps he is screaming inside that that is what he has to do, but his outward persona currently does not allow this. We count 3 clockwise to:

5 Cups Disappointment He shares similar feelings to the woman. Perhaps he is one of those people who always put on a brave face in spite of inner turmoil.

5 Disks Worry He appears to be more pensive than we thought. He is a fire element, but we have not seen a single fire card in this sequence, and nor will we. He is acting, or rather not-acting according to his nature.

6 Swords Science Another card in common. Perhaps they have discussed their problems. They may have tried counselling to understand their marital problems, or perhaps they thought naively that a holiday together would help. The passive nature of the String (only 2 Fire cards and excess Water) does not hold much hope. We then count 6 to:

Hanged Man This completes the sequence on a very downbeat note, which is totally contrary to the positive outlook portrayed by the Knight.

Knight Wands Anticlockwise

The orientation of the Knight suggests anticlockwise is the correct direction, and we see that this sequence is stronger. The Count goes straight onto the Queen, but because she is reversed, the direction does not change. Since the count immediately includes the Queen, we may see this count as representing the both of them. Energetically, this would make sense, as he is the more dynamic of the two, and she would in general follow him. As we will see, familiar cards keep on cropping up.

Queen of Cups He sees her as torn between staying or leaving. Perhaps he is thinking that if they had a break, a trial separation, that things would work out.

5 Disks Worry Worry about the outcome of the relationship.

5 Cups Disappointment Another familiar card.

6 Wands Victory The Queen had this card when we counted anticlockwise for her, but in this situation, the Knight 'owns' it, although fire on fire suggests that he leaps before he looks. He would be thinking in terms of winning, which by definition includes a loser, while she would be trying to find a way out where such an outcome does not have winners or losers.

10 Swords Ruin Here we have confirmation that he will feel victorious, while the Queen will feel she has lost, or that she will feel a failure.

6 Cups Pleasure A positive card, but of course when it is between 6 Wands and the Hanged Man, we have to insert a large note of caution. Perhaps he thinks he can get over the breakup easily and start again, but the 6 Cups 'belongs' to the Queen, as much as the 6 Wands 'belongs' to the Knight. For the breakup to work, both need to feel that they have not lost in the bargain.

Even though the same cards appeared in both sequences for the Knight and the Queen, there is still considerable scope for interpreting those cards differently when required. The top card, the 10 Swords is a powerful indicator of problems, in particular relationships, and we were not disappointed.

Things to do

Try counting from other cards to see the twists and turns, and note how the interpretation of the cards will change. Since there is difference between the various techniques of Pairing and Counting, the question arises as to which is 'correct'. In my experience, it all depends on the situation. Perhaps the Pairings show the 'Fated' direction in the lives of these people, while the Counting gives them mastery of their own direction in life.

Strings, Paths and Highways

After counting from a few cards at random in any String, it quickly comes apparent that there is often a repetition of sequences of cards peculiar to that String, so as soon as these patterns emerge, it is a good idea to stop counting those cards, and look for other cards that follow a different path if that is where the answers lie.

Most cards sequences terminate on one or two cards, while equally, there are cards that seem to go nowhere in particular – the latter group are harder to detect. My initial thought was that the isolated cards had little influence on the reading. However whilst writing this book, all 78 cards in the four sequences were analysed and counted in both directions, the patterns of some of the strings were very strong – one card seemed to be involved in every count.

From there, the next obvious step was to draw up a table that gave the number of hits each card received, and whether it was a terminating card. It then became obvious that diagrams could be created that illustrate the 'isolated' cards as being the seed cards that start the strings; since they were not counted upon, they had to be first.

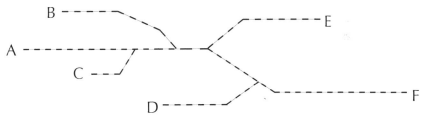

In the diagram above, strings A B and C show the start of the seed cards. A is the ultimate seed card since it is the longest, with B, and then C. D is also a seed card, but it contributory string to the F string. The three strings A B and C converge to have similar cards for a short while until there is a bifurcation to E and F. D is a seed string that starts further down the sequence in the F String, which since it is longest, is the terminating string. Since the Seed cards are easy to miss, they can represent events that were the cause of the current situation, which may or may not be known to the Querent. These Seed cards function in similar ways to the Aces, which are the Roots of the Elements, therefore unmanifest.

CHAPTER SIX

The Hierophant, The Tower, The Sixes and the Princes

The Hierophant = 6, Vau
Taurus, Single Letter

The Tower = 80, Peh
Mars, Double Letter

Establishment versus destruction and chaos. The value of these two cards is 86, which is an important kabbalistic number: ALHYM, Gods (plural), HLLVYH Halleluyah, KVS, cup or chalice, LVYM the Levites, and YH YHVH ADM, The God of Adam.

Tipareth is the centre point of the Tree of Life, and means Beauty. In the Golden Dawn system this is where the Adept can meet his Holy Guardian Angel. This experience can be shattering as easily as illuminating. Once the Adept has met his HGA he has his own authority to act – he has no superiors to defer to. This is probably one of the key reasons why organisations such as the Golden Dawn ran into such factionalising.

The symbol of Tipareth is a young man, which is part of the reason why the Princes are associated with it. In some kabbalistic systems Tipareth is the centre point of Yetsirah, which relates to the element Air. Tipareth is also the junction point of Malkuth and Kether when Trees of Life are daisy-chained together. The polarity of these cards indicates maximum change with maximum stability.

For Crowley, the Hierophant symbolises Horus the Child as God of the new Aeon, born from Nuit (see the Star, previous chapter), which fits in with the symbol of Tipareth. The Hierophant is associated with Taurus, a placid sign, which does not fit well with the martial symbolism of Horus, and it certainly does not match the divinatory meanings of teaching, advice, endurance, orthodoxy, etc.

The aggressive martial qualities are seen in the paired card, the Tower, which is ruled by Mars. Here, the Tower represents the manifestation of cosmic energy in its grossest form. The card depicts the destruction of the old Aeon, so now we see why Crowley intended the Hierophant to be the vehicle for Horus, since it has the qualities of endurance, continuation, etc.

The pairing of opposites reaches its utmost in these two cards, the stability and endurance of the Hierophant with its ultimate materiality of Taurus, and the chaos and destruction of Shiva, which sees any kind of manifestation as a stain on consciousness, which must be annihilated. The magical uses of this powerful combination of cards is clear – removal of the whole system and its replacement with another.

The Sixes

Four sixes indicate pleasure, while three sixes show gain and success.

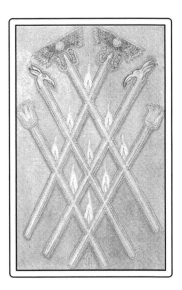

6 Wands, Lord of Victory

The balance between minimal and excessive action is perfect. The 5 Wands is excessive, but the 7 Wands take us into greater imbalance. The Wands of the Three Adepts are burning orderly and steadily.

6 Cups, Lord of Pleasure

The pleasure is harmonized and fertile. This card is one of the best in the Tarot. There is a sense of wellbeing.

6 Swords, Lord of Science

Intelligence is the victor. The Rose Cross appears.

6 Disks, Lord of Success

Harmony and balance in Earth brings success, but these things are temporary. The Rose Cross is fully manifested.

The Princes

4 Princes indicate meeting powerful and influential men, while 3 Princes show rank and position.

The Princes represent the combined forces of their Supernal Parents, so they appear on Chariots. In some respects they counterbalance the upward energies of the Chariot card. The Princes are "the published record of what has been done in secret" (Book of Thoth). In other words, analysis of the position and relationship of the Princes to the other cards can be used to reveal secrets.

Prince of the Chariot of Fire

He is the most reckless of the Princes, inspired by the wisdom of Chokmah, he evangelises. As representative of the Born and Dying God, Crowley associates this card with the Ritual of Christian Rozenkreutz.

Prince of the Chariot of the Waters

As a counter-balance to the Prince of Wands, here we have the secret depths of Binah, the mysteries of birth and death. He is the embodiment of the alchemical qualities of Scorpio.

Prince of the Chariots of the Winds

Crowley mentions a secret crown, which refers to Kether, and indicates the hidden link between it and Tipareth, conjoining Trees of Life from levels above and below. This is almost an intellectual exercise, which has a compelling, if ephemeral truth about it. The ideas are brilliant, but where are the emotions or energy to create something lasting?

Prince of the Chariot of Earth

He symbolises the hard work, the enduring graft, the overcoming of tedium required by the Initiate in order to achieve one's Holy Guardian Angel. The reality is that on the path, glamour is a rare commodity. The card shows the methodical progress from Darkness to Light.

Unaspected Cards

This Chapter is a critical junction point in this book as it marks the point where Divination and Magick unite. The word divination means 'to make divine'. Armed with the technology of Unaspected Cards, the Diviner has the power to connect to his or her Holy Guardian Angel, or learn how the process can be facilitated.

The ability to Card Count adds power to a reading. There are endless subtleties, watching events weave in and out between the main characters, finding dead-ends, then the magic of seeing the new direction appear out of the blue. For years my goal has been to make more Tarot readers aware of the power at their fingertips if they can only make a break from the apparent safety of positional spreads such as the Celtic Cross. Even if Elemental Dignities had not been developed, Card Counting would still be a fantastic method, but at the back of my mind there has been the nagging thought that more is still to be found.

Almost all Tarot readings are done with time constraints, but with this book I had the luxury of spending nearly three months exhaustively analysing the same four Strings of cards. The initial focus was on the lengths of some strings and then the number of times the same cards were 'hit' by the other cards. Anyone who has spent a little time reading Strings using the counting technique will know the feeling when whatever card one starts from, and from either direction, the same card always seems to get hit. By not following the original Golden Dawn rules of only counting from the Significator, the diviner is able to explore multiple timelines to see how a change of direction in the life of the Querent can result in a different outcome – we should all be in control of our destinies.

The problem is that this approach can result in fatalism, which is most unsatisfactory. When life seems to run on tramlines, it is a depressing experience for me, even if the Querent does not feel the same way.

Another problem with looking only at the Significator is that the Reader has no idea where that card appears in a sequence – it could be at the beginning, middle or end. In fact, card counting from only the Significator gives one an outcome, not the provenance or origin.

Another phenomenon is when events appear obvious to the Reader but the Querent is clueless as to what is being talked about. Again, Readers with less confidence might assume faulty technique on their part, but without a proper investigation, there is the entirely reasonable proposition that for whatever reason the Querent really does not know about some events that are happening in his or her life.

My experience has shown that merely following the Strings from whatever card, simply shows up the mundane directions that anybody can take. What about those who desire to follow a spiritual path, ultimately to contact and follow one's Holy Guardian Angel? Counting from a card that is unaspected in both directions (ie: not directly 'hit' in any string) is a powerful indicator of influence from a spiritual agency. Now of course this needs to be qualified since this includes black magic and other practices. For now consider the proposition that the Reader needs to know **where** a string is coming from, and the qualitative decision will come from all the other factors one has to take into account in a reading.

Looked at from a more prosaic perspective, the unaspected cards represent untapped potential within the Querent. It is like a child who wants to ride a bicycle for the first time – it has the motor skills to do this, but they are not co-ordinated, and it takes several attempts and setbacks before the basic skills are mastered. The unaspected cards can also be seen as challenges or areas of life that had not previously been considered. If there is an unaspected Court card, it could represent a person that has not entered the Querent's life or the hidden influence of someone the Querent already knows but had not suspected. In all these cases, the act of drawing attention to the unaspected cards gives the Querent the opportunity to begin to integrate those energies into life.

We can categorise the type of card counts as follows:

1. Cards unaspected from both Clockwise and Anticlockwise
2. Cards unaspected from either Clockwise or Anticlockwise
3. Cards hit from one to three times from either Clockwise or Anticlockwise
4. Cards hit from one to three times both Clockwise and Anticlockwise
5. Cards receiving an average number of hits from both directions
6. Cards receiving significantly high number of hits from one or both directions (Foci cards)

For the purposes of this chapter, only categories 1. and 2. will be considered. The reader is invited to analyse the strings from the point of view of the other categories.

The Supernal Cards and the Holy Guardian Angel

From where do Unaspected cards point from? Since the energies seem to come from outside the system, it could be from another Tree of Life, or from the top of the Tree in the Supernal Triangle, or from the Holy Guardian Angel.

In Kabbalistic terms unaspected cards signify events that are happening at higher levels of the Tree of Life, perhaps at Kether or in the Supernal Triangle. For Magicians aspiring to their Holy Guardian Angel, Card Counting can be used to ascertain either the nature of the Holy Guardian Angel, or the lessons needed to be learned before that experience can be reached. Magicians have tremendous opportunities to harness these energies and direct them as desired, either to manifestation or elsewhere. If a card is unaspected from both directions, it shows events happening at the level of Kether, while if a card is unaspected from the clockwise direction it has influence from Binah, and a card unaspected from the anticlockwise direction has influence from Chokmah. Of course, a card unaspected from one direction has aspects from the other direction, so the unaspected influence is very subtle.

The implications of cards from the Supernal Triangle are profound in magickal terms, for now we can see these cards as representing not only the nature of the magickal operation but how events will unfold and influence the current situation, since we also have the more aspected cards side by side. The ambiguity of the Supernal Triangle is well summed by Crowley in the Book of Thoth, who states that *"for each one containeth in itself its own opposite"*, so while the Supernal Triangle is pure and Holy, we discern not only the development of any Black Magic, but also the antidote to Black Magic.

Influence from Malkuth

The direction of count is significant in terms of how many or how little aspects a card receives. The Anticlockwise direction has such negative connections in terms of black magic or witchcraft, but this need not be so. Some Golden Dawn documents describe the vortex cone of energy emanating from Malkuth of a higher Tree of Life to Kether of a Tree below. In that case, evil intent will not be present. The String of cards is laid out in a line or horseshoe, so circularity is not so evident. A better way of understanding the direction is in terms of the Chokmah and Binah, represented by Knight and Queen respectively. The Knight is the activating intelligence, while the Queen is receptive and consolidating, and we can also include the level of the String, so card counts clockwise in the Air String would represent the energies of the Queen of Swords, while anticlockwise counting of the Water String would have qualities of the Knight of Cups.

Levels of Creation

At this point, it would be useful to consider one version of the levels of Creation within the Tree of Life. The four levels of creation corresponding to the four elements are: Atziluth, Briah, Yetsirah and Assiah. The highest level of Atziluth corresponds to Fire, and is found only in Kether. Briah represents Water, Chokmah and Binah, while the next six Sephiroth are Air and represent Yetsirah, and finally, Assiah represents Earth, and Malkuth. The Aces and Court cards parallel these levels: Aces – Kether, Knights and Queens (Chokmah and Binah) – Briah; Princes – Yetsirah (Tipareth); and the Princesses – Malkuth and Assiah.

Thus, from a practical point of view we can immediately assign influence from the card counts. Categories 1 to 4 above represent the Supernal Triangle; Category 5 represent Yetsirah, while the high counts of Category 6 represent Assiah.

Levels of creation can be nested within each other, so Atziluth, Briah, Yetsirah and Assiah will be found in Atziluth, and so on. The structure of the four sets of Court cards accurately reflects this in their elemental structure. The various commentaries on the court cards found within the Book of Thoth are most illuminating, particularly in the Fool chapter.

Kabbalistic doctrine states that the highest levels are not available to all but the most spiritually advanced Kabbalist, which I find perfectly acceptable. The reading of the tarot to the general public is a democratising process, and while I do not believe the Tarot can be used to determine the level of spirituality that the client is functioning at, there is no reason to suppose that it is not possible for a tarot reader who has not reached the higher levels to discern where the influence from a particular level is coming from. After all, the four Strings of cards representing the four elements are in the YHVH order which represents those same four levels of creation! So, unaspected cards in the Fire String represent the Supernal Triangle of Atziluth; the Supernal Triangle of Briah for the Water String; the Supernal Triangle of Yetsirah in the Air String, and the Supernal Triangle for Assiah in the Earth String.

If the number or lack of card counts represents the levels of creations, then we have a spacetime model for that person since the elements are represented in the vertical and horizontal directions. Events (Zero counts) higher up the Tree can be considered as unmanifest or in the future, so a magician or kabbalist who effects change at those levels can be considered to be changing the future. There is a reciprocal effect going on – by changing space, time will be influenced, and vice versa, so if the client changes direction as a result of the tarot consultation, events can be influenced.

Alternatively, events can either be speeded up or delayed. The sequence of Tarot cards presented to the Querent shows the possibilities for change **if desired**. At the quantum level, the effect of the observer is profound, and has to be included in the calculations. So simple meditation by the Querent and/or the Tarot Reader on those cards that are unaspected can produce powerful and profound change. One way to do this is to highlight those cards by raising them out of the sequence so they stand proud. Alternatively, a list of those cards can be made, and they can be grouped together on an altar or other sacred space. The kabbalistic correspondences of the cards can also be considered – the possibilities are endless. One word of warning – when dealing with higher levels of creation, the imagery on tarot cards is far less important, so I would suggest the traditional images of the Sephiroth to be used, and they are found in Dion Fortune's *The Mystical Qabalah.*

Thus far we have considered sequences of cards in terms of number of aspects, so now it is time to consider fully formed Sequences. The diagram on page 73 of the Strings shows how a Tree formation can be created, with branches at the top, the main trunk, and the root. The beginnings of the branches show the starts of the card counts and how they merge into the main trunk. The trunk shows the repeating patterns of the cards and some of these cards will also terminate some of the sequences, but one card at the end will be the final terminating card.

All of this represents a fairly solid structure, the path of which the Querent is happy to follow, but the reader familiar with kabbalistic theory knows that the level of Malkuth and the Princesses is anything but fixed, and the energy can easily move up the Tree of Life to either Kether or Binah, depending on the system used. Of course, where the main sequences of cards representing this Tree are entirely congenial, there is no reason to change anything. Apart from the fortunate outcomes to reading, the Reader will have to exercise some judgement as to whether alternative futures are viable.

My own study and experience over the years has led me to the conclusion that anything is possible – anything can be changed. The desirability of that change, the effort required to make that change, and the knock on effects of making that change often mitigate any such effort. Armed with the knowledge that change is always possible and the Querent is prepared to believe that life is not as fatalistic the effect of a Tarot reading should be to uplift and inspire.

Instead of seeing card counting as the means to divine one approach to how events will unfold, with some diligence the enterprising Tarot Reader will not only be able to present alternative views of how the future will unfold, but provide mechanisms for making the future (and the past) different. Those cards that have one or two aspects are not as flexible as those that are unaspected, but they can still be influenced.

As we shall see, knowledge of the unaspected cards would have made some difference as to what was said during the consultation. Tarot cards associated with the Supernal Triangle do not seem to have the negative connotations they would have in other circumstances. Since events are happening within the Supernal Triangle, we do not need to consider Elemental Dignities.

Used properly the arrow of time is obvious in counting sequences – we have a beginning, middle and end, but when we consider sequences starting from unaspected cards, we see that they either have not happened yet, or are at a more formative stage. As we will see, this distinction is useful when separating out groups of Court cards.

Unaspected cards in the Fire String

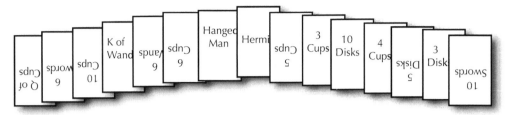

The 10 Cups and 3 Disks are completely unaspected, and serve as a balance to the ruinous 10 Swords top card. Referring back to Chapter One, we saw that this String concerned an apparently locked relationship between a man and woman. The woman seemed to desire escape, but she was unable to change circumstances. In the anticlockwise direction, the Queen and 10 Swords are part of the group with the most aspects, while in the clockwise direction she is locked in an eternal embrace with the Knight.

As unaspected cards in the Fire String, the 10 Cups and 3 Disks are associated with the Ace of Wands, new beginnings, so meditation on either of these cards would be desirable. Previous analyses of this String had not shown any real escape for these people. Note how the 3 Disks is surrounded by the 5 Disks and 10 Swords who both have very high aspect counts.

The clockwise count reveals the Hermit as another unaspected card, which suggests that change may happen in September (Virgo, and thus September, is associated with this card). The clockwise count is associated with the Queen, so we might infer that she should be patient and make plans, or that she could do self-development work in the meantime.

Anticlockwise, we have the 10 Disks, Knight Wands, 3 Cups and the Hanged Man unaspected. The Knights are associated with anticlockwise counts, and this card rules the count in the Fire String. However, the card count for the Knight takes us immediately onto the Queen, so energetically, she takes the energy. If we count the 'wrong' way round for the Knight, we hit the Hanged Man, but it is only counting anticlockwise that the Hanged Man is unaspected. With ordinary card counting, we would have had problems seeing what the Knight is up to, but now see that he is biding his time (Hanged Man), and he intends to enjoy (3 Cups) himself in the meantime.

The unaspected cards in the Fire String show opportunities for change. The Hanged Man and Hermit show the need for introspection, and the ability to act secretly.

CHAPTER SEVEN

The Lovers, The Devil and the Sevens

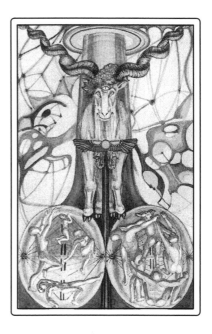

VI The Lovers = 7, Zayin
Air, Gemini, Single Letter

XV The Devil = 70, Ayin
Earth, Capricorn, Single Letter

77 is one less than the number of Tarot cards, which is what it would be if we counted the Fool card as Zero. The Gematria is interesting; BOH is prayed, GYChVN the River Gihon (Genesis ii.13), ZYDVN Overflowing, MGDL Towers, Citadels, MZL the influence from Kether, OZ Strength, a he goat.

The Lovers card represents the concept that there should be equilibrium and harmony, so that the opposite idea should always be present. Solve et coagula or Analysis then Synthesis represents this idea. Crowley explicitly links the Lovers to the Magus card, not just because Mercury rules Gemini. He sees the card as "the Creation of the World", where the voice of the Magus commands it. The marriage represented is of the Emperor and Empress, while the winged Orphic egg represents the colours of the Supernal Triangle.

AYN means an eye, which also appears on the Tower card. Capricorn and Pan rule high places, hence the gematria for Towers, Citadels, and of course, OZ, strength, for the Goat, symbol of Capricorn. This card represents the application of Will, whose successful application will result in Victory, the nature of Netzach. The two cards together suggest that the application of will in the analysis and synthesis of a situation will prevail, but of course the Lovers represents concepts relating to alchemy and the Great Work, so there has to be a union between subtlety of mind and the overwhelming will and aspiration to achieve the goal.

The Sevens

The Seven's represent problems the client or querent has to overcome in any situation – look at the surrounding cards for clues. Netzach means Victory, which is the achievement after effort. 4 Sevens indicate disappointments (Devil), while 3 Sevens show contracts or treaties (Lovers).

Frequently, where the Seven's predominate there is a feeling of being overwhelmed, of not seeing the wood for the trees, and a total collapse of will. The things that we have to overcome in life and on the spiritual are different for all of us, but the lesson is that we have to keep going. We also need to understand that while the obstacles in life we are required to overcome are always within our abilities, we tend to take on challenges that are nothing to do with us, obscuring the path, making it farther away than it should be.

The magical image of Netzach is of a beautiful naked woman, which does not exactly convey the concept of victory, except perhaps in seduction. Venus is associated with this sephira, so the notion of victory is in seeing the higher aspects

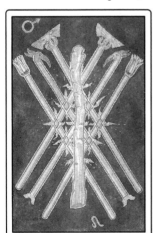

of love, to go beyond exterior form of beauty, and see things at a greater depth of insight. The prominence and popularity of pornography on the internet is a good example of how far away this victory can be.

7 Wands, Lord of Valour

The energy is almost depleted – it is only one's sense of honour that keeps things going.

7 Cups, Lord of Debauch

This is the card of delusion, falling into false pleasure.

7 Swords, Lord of Futility

The energy is weaker than the 7 Wands, amounting not much more than aspiration, but even that has doubts. The expectation is of the failure in the 7 Disks.

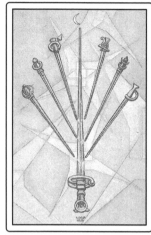

7 Disks, Lord of Failure

Total capitulation; there is not even an attempt to remedy the situation due to total passivity.

Love Relationships

Ask any Tarot reader what question is asked most in a reading, and relationships will be at the top of the list. As well as personal ones, there is also the relationship between the self and the Higher Self. The chief aim of the Adepts of the Golden Dawn was and is the Knowledge and Conversation with one's Holy Guardian Angel. Modern expressions are Higher Self or Higher Intuition. Mysticism has Union with God as its aim. All of these terms define a relationship between man or woman and higher levels of consciousness.

As you have seen in the examples, the Card Counting techniques are exemplary in analysing the interrelationships between cards, and one can follow threads showing how the Court cards converge, separate, maintain parallel courses, argue, work together, and fall in love. We can see hidden agendas and other people interfering.

We use the system of Elemental Dignities to analyse the relationship between the cards. Elemental Dignities is based upon the Dialectic, which concerns the relationship between God and Man. The Dialectic is about the relationship between opposing forces that creates a third force. We see this in sex where the union of two people traditionally creates a child. Sex can cement a relationship, or it can cause it to fail. Where the intention is not to create a child in the traditional sense, something is always created at higher levels, so it is important that the couple are clear about what they are creating – the technical term is "Magical Child". Aleister Crowley wrote extensively on the subject, and his novel *Moonchild* concerns the creation of a magical child.

Compatibility

Just as astrology uses compatibility techniques to determine the success or failure of a relationship, with the Opening of the Key Spread, the interaction between the Court cards, representing the people in the relationship, can be analysed using various methods. In the reading below, most of the in-depth analysis was not done at the time, but the reader will note that these methods support an intuitive analysis.

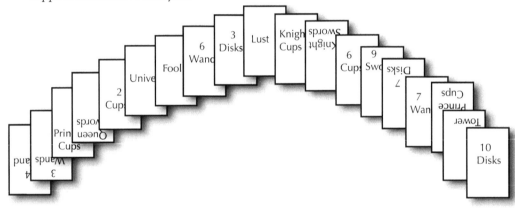

The Querent was a woman who wished to know whether her current love affair would work. As we will see, she will soon have a better opportunity coming along. In analysing the Overview, we will be following the methods covered in Chapter One, but in the original reading the focus was primarily on the court cards. Full use of all of the techniques is useful not only as an exercise but as part of the preparation for a magical ritual. However, in this case only the Water Pile was recorded in detail.

Since the reading was performed, many of the details have come true. Tarot readers often have little time to record or analyse a reading to the depths contained in these chapters, particularly since the general drift of the reading comes to light quickly. When I was discussing analysing the finer points of taking into account all other cards in the reading with another Tarot reader, he admitted that he would suggest that the other cards represented 'noise'! In many respects I have to agree with him. With these techniques we have the opportunity to see if our intuition matches the various methods of analysis.

Top Card

The top card is the 10 Disks, financial gain, which is sympathetic to the Water Pile. The Tower card is adjacent, which is a worry, while on the other side is the 4 Wands – both cards surrounding the 10 Disks are friendly to the Earth card, but they are weakened when related to the Water Pile.

Number of Cards

There are 19 cards, which relates to the 19th Major card, the Moon, Deception. In this reading only the Water Pile was considered, and we do not have a record of the positions of the other cards so cannot see how the Moon might relate to the Water String.

Centre Card

The centre card is Lust, which as a Fiery card, is weakened by the Water pile, relating to passion and desire, so there may have been some uncertainty as to whether the woman really wanted love in her life. This may reflect the influence of the Moon card above. When counting clockwise, no card 'hits' the Lust card, which suggests a loose cannon, there is nothing to moderate it, but when counting cards anticlockwise, there are seven 'hits'.

Major/Minor/Court Cards balance

There are slightly more Court cards than Major cards, which is significant, so people are able to change their destiny, particularly as the number of Minor cards is one more than the Court cards and Major cards combined.

Three or Four of a Kind

There are no Three or Four of a kind.

Tree of Life

The absence of Aces, 5's and 8's shows that none of the three triangles on the Tree of Life are complete. Lack of Aces suggests either disconnection (Kether is the origin or beginning of any process), or that the processes that started the current situation had happened previously. The lack of 5's or 8's remove most of the Pillar of Severity which shows that maybe the desire for change has not been very strong, since the Fives represent the transformation of settled situations. The missing 8's represent communication, so perhaps there have either been communication problems, or that the Querent desires a relationship that works on the mental level.

The weak Pillar of Severity means that there would be a natural desire to remain with the status quo, represented by Chesed. Some of the Major cards that connect to Kether, Geburah and Hod are found in the Water String, which could be seen as the desire to fully connect up the paths. The Fool card, which is on the path between Kether and Chokmah, would be the desire to connect to the source, which seems to be missing, since there are no Aces.

The only two is the 2 Cups, and we already know the topic of the reading is love, but we have the Knight of Cups and Knight of Swords who also represent Chokmah. The Lust card is on the reciprocating path between Chesed and Geburah. Below and parallel to the Lust path is the Tower card, connecting the missing 8s to the 7s, which suggests to me that coupled with the uncertainty of change is the fear that repeating mistakes from previous relationships will happen again (the Tower card often represents events from the past).

The path between missing Geburah and Hod is the Hanged Man, sacrifice and loss. Unfortunately, a record of the other Piles was not kept, so we cannot see how the sacrifice and loss would have been represented elsewhere in the reading. There is good news, in that the Universe, connecting Yesod and Malkuth is present; the path from 9 Swords Cruelty to 10 Disks Wealth, shows that the outcome is excellent.

Reversals

Three of the Court cards are reversed, which suggests some kind of connection between them. Only the Knight Cups is upright. The other reversed cards are fairly randomly distributed.

Elemental Imbalances

Fire slightly dominates, but it is weakest in the Water Pile – otherwise, the elements are well balanced.

Pairing Overview

The pairing goes from the 10 Disks/4 Wands to Lust. The outside pairing does not suggest romance, but in terms of the overall picture, it could be that the successful relationship might have either a work or business connection. Below is an analysis of the paired cards.

4 Wands (reversed): Completion and 10 Disks: Wealth

This combination suggests a business deal that could be financially advantageous.

3 Wands (reversed): Virtue and The Tower (reversed)

Sudden changes in actions or career, but note that these fire cards are in the Water pile, so we would not expect change to happen quickly.

Princess Cups and Prince Cups (reversed)

A younger woman who does not appreciate the advances of a man.

Queen Swords (reversed) and 7 Wands: Valour

The woman is a fighter.

2 Cups (reversed): Love and 7 Disks (reversed): Failure

She wants love, but she either does not expect to find it, or that it will work for her.

The Universe and 9 Swords: Cruelty

Confirmation that she expects the desired outcome to fail. The Universe represents the matter at hand, and the outcome, while very little good comes from the 9 Swords.

Fool and 6 Cups: Pleasure

The Fool represents beginnings, but from an unexpected source, so while she is expecting relationships to fail, perhaps the focus is on enjoyment, rather than relationships.

6 Wands: Victory and Knight Swords (reversed)

An intelligent man who wants to succeed, and perhaps inspire her. The Knight is the Fool in the previous pairing, so perhaps she meets him in a situation where pleasure and enjoyment predominates. This man likes to win, and he does things his own way, or he is self-made, since the 6 Wands is a minor card.

3 Disks: Work and Knight Cups

He also enjoys working, perhaps is self-employed. It is possible that she discovers that her work interests coincide with his work interests.

Lust

The Lust card is a good indicator of a passionate love affair. This will be the key card to any magical action. In the context of the water stack we see that there may be a psychic attachment or understanding between the two.

Summary

Note that the mood of the pairing changes dramatically after the Universe and 9 Swords, and we identified this combination with the 10 Disks as suggesting a positive outcome. It is only when she gives up that circumstances improve in ways she could never imagine. We see the Prince of Cups as the old, failed love, while the new man will be the Knight of Swords, whom she sees as intelligent and articulate who looks at life differently. After a short while she sees him in a more romantic light as the Knight of Cups, and they could work together. When we card count, we should be able to discern the difference.

Analysing the entire set of counting sequences, we see that the Knight of Swords has no interaction with the other cards, which suggests that he is entirely new to the situation. He has nothing to do with this woman's previous relationships, and it is too early to see exactly how he will act in the future, which is consonant with the Fool card.

The 'busiest' cards are the 4 Wands and 3 Disks, indicating hard work is the real focus of life at the moment. Cards with low counts are the 6 Cups, Pleasure, showing that there is not much of that going on, while the 10 Disks suggests that wealth has not arrived yet. The 7 Disks is completely isolated, so nobody wants to do the work expected of them.

Elemental Dignities

Before we look at the Card Counting, an analysis of the elements will give us an idea of what is going on between the cards.

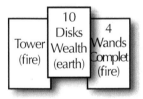

Fears about financial security at work, or starting any new venture, or there have been some sudden changes at work. Either that or a lot of pressure is experienced at work. Note that although the original question was about love, it does not seem that this woman is looking for a rich man! All tens have an indeterminate quality about them, and this one is no exception. Note that if you count ten from the top card in one direction, you will hit the Lust card, which we have already highlighted. Elementally, the cards are friendly, although rather heavy.

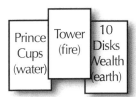

Three different elements, and we see that the Earth card is strongest, balancing the fire and water. Our analysis from the Pairing shows that the Prince of Cups represents either present or past love; the Tower indicates he may be the old love.

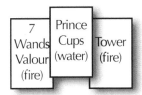

The prince is really very weak, possibly fearful, a loser. He may be unable to take pressure.

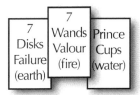

The two sevens show problems to overcome. There could be a pattern of failure both with this man and with the woman. The Earth card is strongest since it is friendly to fire and water, but the pattern is still passive.

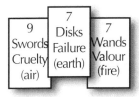

The picture gets worse. Now the Fire card is strongest, but there is no emotion or feeling. Perhaps all the underlying issues never got discussed.

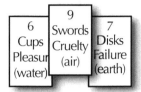

A positive card, which is friendly with Air and Earth, in contrast to the previous set of three cards.

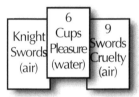

It is possible that the woman consulted this man for advice on relationships. He is fun to talk to, but has known sorrow too.

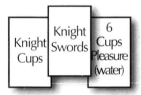

Either we have two men, or the same person. Possibly he is hard to pin down, or he has an elusive quality. There must be some fascination. The cards have become more emotional.

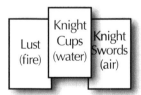

Ordinarily, we would see Fire next to Water as not a good combination, but we are considering the possibility that the two Knights represent one person. The Knight of Cups is next to the Lust card, which has been identified as having a magical use.

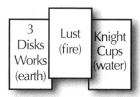

The Earth card balances the other two. We can see the 3 Disks as the beginning of a new venture, either of love or work.

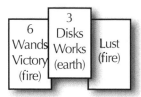

These cards show new beginnings, success and victory. Earth and Fire are friendly, and overall, the triplet is dynamic.

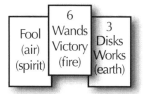

The Fool represents events from an unusual quarter or in an unusual manner. Next to Victory, we would see that victory either as unusual or unusual in the manner of execution.

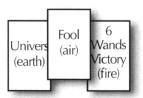

Endings and Beginnings, or revolving doors are indicated, still with that success.

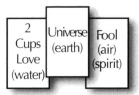

The Universe card is described by Aleister Crowley as "The matter of the question itself, synthesis... the crystallization of the whole matter involved." The 2 cups is of course about love, while the Fool card represents beginnings from unexpected sources. The Universe card can indicate foreign influence.

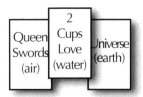

We can see these cards as indicating that the woman will initiate the relationship. The water card is the strongest card.

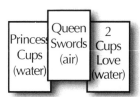

She presents herself as cool, calm, level headed, but underneath, she is passionate.

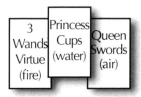

The Queen is strongest elementally, with affinities to the 3 Wands, so perhaps there are problems with a younger woman at work.

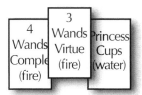

Perhaps she feels overworked? The Fire swamps the water card.

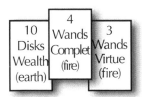

A hard working, successful situation, that eventually arises after some inertia, shown by the two reversed cards.

Card Counting

There are several approaches to reading this set of cards. We will begin with the 10 Disks as that is the top card, then we will use the Queen Swords as signifying the client, or we could look at the love interest. When she came for the reading, she wanted to know if the relationship with the current man would work. He seems to be the Prince of Cups, and Fire cards, not good auspices, surround him. It is always a good idea to get a feel for the cards; get an overview with the top card, look at cards that could represent the Querent, and then focus on the reason for the reading. Conveniently, all these aspects can often be seen from the first card we count from, but not in this reading. We will have to dig deeper. Some of the three card groups will be counted several times in different strings, so note how the interpretation of the three card groups changes according to context. Here is where the skill of the Tarot Reader in blending the disparate threads into a coherent story comes into play.

10 Disks anticlockwise

The focus of the top card is money worries to do with the past (Tower reversed), with more than a suggestion of overwork. The Querent might be asking about love, but maybe she needs to change her work patterns. We then count ten to:

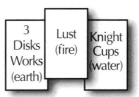

Lust is the centre card, which is significant in itself. The Knight is also working hard. He is not sure about passion (Fire and Water are enemies), so he prefers work. We count twelve to:

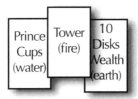

There has been a financial crisis for the Prince. Counting nine, this sequence ends as it returns to the Lust card.

This is a very short loop. See how there is no female interest here? The Knight Cups preoccupation is with work and money. He could have financial problems, or he is worried about financial information leaking out. Perhaps he cannot afford his overdraught. The appearance of the Prince Cups could be a younger rival, but again this could be more to do with work. An alternative explanation for these cards could simply be the office politics where the Querent works.

10 Disks clockwise

Count ten to:

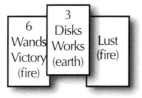

Two fire cards surrounding an earth card, showing the focus is still on career and work, but in the second triplet the fire cards are now very positive and not backward looking at all. Also, none of the cards are reversed. We count 3 to:

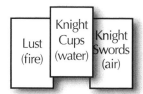

The focus switches to relationships. Lust is next to the Knight Cups, the love interest, but of course in Elemental Dignity terms, these cards are weakened, being Fire and Water. The Knight Swords is interesting as he is the strongest card. The Knight Cups switches direction to:

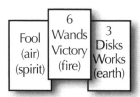

The Fool card is the only new card to interpret here. The action for the 10 Disks centres on the Lust triplet going one way, and, going the other way, the six card series; Fool, 6 Wands, 3 Disks, Lust, Knight Cups, Knight Swords. So in one direction the new man comes into the picture, but not the other.

The Fool of course represents something new happening from an unexpected direction, and since the Knight Swords has been peripheral in this card counting, I would suggest he is connected with the Fool. On the other side of the Fool is the Universe, so we have beginnings and endings, and in my experience, the Universe can indicate foreign places.

Perhaps the Knight Swords is foreign – in any event he would not be someone she usually takes an interest in. I have been talking about the Knight Swords, but remember that it is the Knight Cups that changed the direction of the count, so it is possible he did something to change the perceptions of the Querent. We count six onto:

Using elemental dignities, we know that the Queen is strongest since she is friendly with the other two elements. In the Book of Thoth, the 3 Wands "represents the establishment of primeval Energy." To me, what has been established here is the presence of the mysterious Knight of Swords. If we had only looked at the 10 Disks, this is the first indication of the significator of the Querent, and of course we have a choice. I would opt for the Queen Swords since she would then have an affinity with the Knight Swords, even though the Knight Cups changed the direction of the count. Another interpretation would be that the Querent is at a crossroads – she could either be the Princess or the Queen. The Princess is in charge of the count, and she reverses the direction back to the 3 Disks.

Evidently, the Princess has the upper hand, and work seems to be the focus – she has evaded the issue! Since we have already hit the 3 Disks, and from the same direction despite the two direction changes, the counting stops here. When we counted in the opposite direction, the count stopped on Lust.

Even though counting from the top card, the 10 Disks, introduced the main characters of the reading, we are no closer to knowing what advice to give to the Querent, or even what she is likely to do, except overwork, and she wants to know about love.

From the general description of the man in her life, it would seem that the Prince of Cups fits the bill. Interestingly, except for the reversed Tower card (not a good omen!) and the Queen Swords, none of his counted cards intersects with those of the 10 Disks.

Prince Cups

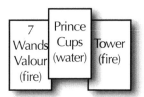

The Prince is sandwiched between two fire cards that are overwhelming the water card. He feels that he can never overcome events, so either ignores them, or he stays in the past. There is still an intensity of feeling. Taking the 10 Disks as representing the general overview, we see that the Prince and Tower cards are reversed. I find the reversed Tower usually represents upsets from the past. The Prince might not feel like history, but perhaps he represents some unresolved issues from her past. The Prince is reversed, so we count four to the Right, which takes us to:

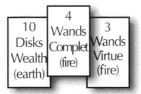

Not exactly love cards are they? Hard work is probably the biggest priority for him, so he does not have to face his problems. The two fire cards can represent the unfinished business suggested by the fire cards from the previous three cards.

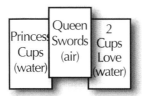

Now we see what he has been avoiding – two women from his past. Counting four we arrive at the client's significator, a good sign, but note that she is reversed, so we count back to the 4 and then the Prince of Cups. This is a locked situation.

We had the Princess of Cups taking charge in the 10 Disks, but here it is the Queen, so we should look at her next.

Queen Swords

This card is reversed, and we know that counting in this direction will result in hitting the Prince of Cups, so we need to go 4 in the other direction to the:

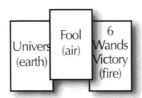

If she takes the new steps she will be successful. She has to realise that she needs to change her life completely, and of course in our analysis of the 10 Disks, we identified the Fool as possibly connected to the Knight Swords. The counting in this direction for the Queen follows closely that of the 10 Disks, which strongly suggests to me that she has been going in the wrong direction with the Prince Cups.

We count 3 from the Fool to:

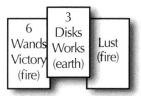

Another positive set of cards, and note how the 6 Wands connects the two triplets containing Lust and the Fool together.

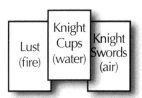

The change she makes in her life brings her into contact with the new man who is serious and professional, but great fun to be with. The direction of the count changes, and takes us to:

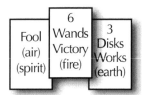

New opportunities present themselves in ways she had not thought of.

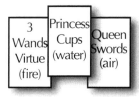

We now see that the Princess could in fact represent her. She is starting a new life, and feels younger. The direction changes and we count 7 to the 3 Disks. We have already come across this card, but from the other direction, so technically, we would need to continue card counting, but from the 3 Disks we go to the Knight of Cups, which is definitely the end of the line.

The contrast between the Prince of Cups and the Knight of Swords is so marked, that I would advise the client to look in an entirely new direction, which takes her to the Knight.

Unaspected Cards

The unaspected cards clockwise are:

- 2 Cups
- Lust
- Knight Swords
- 7 Wands
- 10 Disks

As we already know, the 10 Disks is the top card of the String, and it represents an overview of the reading. None of the cards are adjacent, so we do not have to be so rigorous with Elemental Dignities, which means that the meanings of these cards naturally suggests a passionate man (Lust), who has principles (7 Wands), is looking for love (2 Cups), and has money (10 Disks). At the time of writing, the Querent seems to have found this man, and the only wrong prediction is that he is not wealthy.

The unaspected cards anticlockwise are:

- 3 Wands
- Knight Swords
- 6 Cups
- 7 Disks
- 7 Wands

Comparing them with the unaspected clockwise cards we see that the Knight Swords and 7 Wands appear in both, and see how they hit exactly the same cards in exactly the same sequence in the anticlockwise count. Counting from the Knight we hit the Fool, 2 Cups and Queen Swords, which gives us confirmation that the Knight Swords is the new man in her life. Although Elemental Dignities should not be given too much prominence here, it is noteworthy that the Knight is friendly with all the cards except the 7 Disks.

CHAPTER EIGHT

The Chariot, Temperance (Art) and the Eights

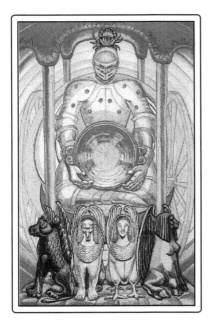

The Chariot = 8, Cheth
Water, Cancer, Single Letter

Temperance or Art = 60, Samehk
Fire, Sagittarius, Single Letter

68 has values of ChLL emptiness, ChS silence, NBYAH prophetess, SDD to shut up, and Binah. The Eighth Sephira of the Tree of Life is Hod which is associated with Mercury, and has kabbalistic connotations of prophecy.

The Chariot brings down the Water from Binah; the canopy is the blue of Binah, while the scarlet wheels represent fiery Geburah. Four sphinxes draw the chariot where the elements are counter changed to represent the 16 sub-elements. So despite the original influence of Binah and Geburah, we have an entirely balanced elemental disposition. In the Golden Dawn system, and in this book, the balanced appearance of all four elements is a powerful spiritual base for change, and is represented as the God Osiris. This is important, because the Chariot is the means of ascent through the heavenly planes, and is inspired by the Mercaba vision in Ezekiel 1, Chapter 1.

Unless the four elements are totally balanced within the individual, there is great danger when engaging in spiritual practices. There are several rituals one can do to remedy this, such as the Lesser Banishing Ritual and the Greater Banishing Ritual, and to work through the Grades of the Golden Dawn. Another method is to use the techniques described in this book so that the elements are experienced regularly.

Frieda Harris works into the frieze of the canopy the word "Abracadabra". Crowley mentions use of the word ABRAHADABRA as the word of the Aeon. Maybe Crowley's eyesight was failing, but since Frieda helped on the proof reading of the Book of Thoth, it is a surprising inconsistency. The important point here is that Abrahadabra is related to Binah, not Hod, so it would be the word uttered by the Magus that creates the worlds, and so we almost have a paradox in that the Chariot is the means to travel through the planes, and it has the Word to create those realms. In other words, the Chariot is the means to connect the sephirah Hod with the Magus via the word Abrahadabra.

Since the Moon rules Cancer, Crowley observes similarities to the High Priestess, which is not surprising since this card is concerned with travel and ascent through the planes. Hod and Netzach are the prime sephiroth concerned with prophecy and spiritual visions, but it is noticeable in the Bible that not only did many prophecies not come true (ignoring the obvious political manipulation of events so that they appear to fulfil predictions), but that the populace generally ignored the imprecations of the prophets and carried on their sinful ways. For me, the concept of prophecy is not that predictions can be made, but that utterances or prophecies are made when an individual is in an ecstatic state when connected to higher spiritual levels. The true function of a prophet is to connect the higher with the lower, to be a conduit of spiritual energy from God (or whoever you want to call him) to the individual.

Hod is connected to Mercury, which of course relates to the Magus where the Word was uttered. Writers such as Kenneth Grant have argued about which Word is supposed to be the Word of the New Aeon, but here I am concerned with the mechanics of how one can find one's own word of the New Aeon, since an individual New Aeon seems more likely than the New Aeon for the entire world.

The Gematria value of 68 is most instructive in this context, for it describes the state one must be in to prophecy. The emptiness of ChLL, the silence of ChS and SDD, to shut up, show that intense meditation is required, and that all thoughts of the mundane world are silenced, possibly with periods of isolation. This book is not intended to be a manual of meditation, but there are some practises that will facilitate the process of meditation here. The writings of Aryeh Kaplan are most instructive; he has reconstructed Kabbalistic methods of meditation similar to that found in India. ChS silence is the combination of the Chariot and Temperance, so we may conclude that the combination of these cards would be a powerful indicator of profound spiritual knowledge that may become available.

Temperance or Art is considered by Crowley to be intimately connected to the Lovers card, which is interesting in the light of the above since Mercury rules Gemini. Whereas the Chariot card has all four elements permuted correctly (a hint that in some cases this is enough to cause ecstatic travel), the Art card shows how to transpose and transmute the elements.

In the Chariot, the body is the means of travel, while in this card, the arrow of Will or Thelema, is a symbol of Mercury. Both cards symbolise the ability to travel in spirit, and to gather information. The Art card is the continuation of the Royal Marriage started in the Lovers card, but now the equilibrium and counter change of the elements happens within the figures, as opposed to between them. The workings of the four elements are seen in their alchemical context unified with the workings on the Tree of Life. For example, Fire and Water mingle harmoniously at the bottom of the card, and they are also the elements of the Pillars of Severity and Mercy respectively, which are united in the Middle Pillar. It is noteworthy that both these cards are associated with vertical Paths, the Art card being between Yesod, the Moon and Tiphareth the Sun, while the Chariot connects the Fire of Geburah with the Waters of Binah.

Crowley sees the Huntress Diana (note the bow on the knees of the High Priestess) as symbolic of the Archer, a description of Sagittarius. Astrologically, Sagittarius is related to the Guru, Higher Knowledge and foreign travel, while Cancer represents the home and conveyances.

Alchemically, the Art card represents the contents of the Orphic egg found in the Lovers card, representing the final stages of the Great Work. Just as in the Chariot we have a magical word in the cape of the Chariot, in the Art card we have VITRIOL found in the cape of the figure; the Universal Solvent, or Visita Interiora Terrae Rectificando Invenies Occultum Lapidem; "Visit the interior parts of the earth; by rectification thou shalt find the hidden stone'. Crowley focuses on the hidden stone as a universal medicine, but here I shall mention some significant Kabbalistic concepts that could equally apply. "Rectification' is a word similar to Tikkun, a technique of restoration of the cosmic realms or the individual

We can see this card as representing the marriage between the Bride of Microprosopos, Shekinah (Malkuth, the earth) and Zeir Anpin the Son, represented by Tiphareth.

Now we can see both cards as signifying the ability to travel the cosmic realms, the Chariot representing the body which has been elementally balanced, allied with the Art card representing the Will which has dynamically balanced the opposites. With the Will working at this level the marriage between Shekinah and Zeir Anpin takes place resulting in a correction of the universes.

The Eights

4 Eights indicate news, while 3 Eights indicate travel (Chariot).

8 Wands, Lord of Swiftness
Fire has been purified and exalted.

8 Cups, Lord of Indolence
Lack of action as the result of unfulfilled expectations.

8 Swords, Lord of Interference
Unforeseen bad luck or trivial incidents knock plans out of kilter.

8 Disks, Lord of Prudence
Strength in inaction, waiting to harvest the planted seed.

Performing Readings for the Public

The Opening of the Key Spread is considered to be the Crown of the Golden Dawn tarot system, suitable only for Adepts. However, the practice and techniques developed in the previous lessons are sufficient for you to start reading the Opening of the Key Tarot Spread not only with confidence, but you will be reading this spread better than most experts.

The Spread is also a magical ritual designed to put the Reader and the Querent in a state conducive to the reception of information. In the Golden Dawn, the reading was preparation for Conversation with one's Holy Guardian Angel, but this is largely irrelevant when performing readings for the public. Whatever the intention, tarot readings should be conducted in a dedicated space, and with time, a definite aura becomes discernable.

Traditional books on magic and divination from both the East and West give authoritative – and differing – advice, on the topology, direction, and time of day, and the weather for optimum results. Significance is also given to omens seen on the way to the place of divination. While this all smacks of superstition, you might like to keep an eye out for the unusual event and see if it is indicative of anything. I doubt my office on Brighton beach fulfils many of the requirements, particularly as I am open for work most days, and I have started readings during all kinds of supposedly bad omens, void of course moons and any other negative omens with no bad effects. I have also gone to work with the most positive omens possible, and still had an awful day. We cannot control the external events, but we control the environment the reading takes place.

Professional readers like me have a room or office for this purpose, but whether you lay the cards out on the carpet, the coffee table, or an altar, it is a good idea to perform some kind of purification at the start of the day, and at the end, and in some cases, between clients. The burning of incense or Native American smudge sticks is a good idea, as is a banishing ritual using the pentagram or hexagram. On my desk I have a small statue of Buddha, and statues of Gods from other religions as well as some other artefacts. Dim lighting is also conducive. The use of such paraphernalia helps not only the Reader, but also the querent, who should feel that s/he is entering a different place to the norm. Some Tarot Readers dress up. I don't, and there again, some people walk in the office surprised to see a man sitting there, despite the large signs saying "Paul Hughes-Barlow".

There are Eastern books that give advice on the significance of whether the querent leads with the right or left leg, or raises the right or left hand. You may wish to experiment here. Swara Yoga, the science of breath, analyses the type of divination according to which tattwa predominates, when the right or left nostril is active when the client walks in, or when the question is asked, or the divination commences (see Harish Johari's books on the subject). Having said all this, there are days when every client is moving house, or getting a new job, going through a divorce etc, there are days when every client is a joy, and there are days when every reading is a nightmare. That is what makes the job (and it is a job, believe me), so fascinating and enriching.

The mental state of Reader and Querent is important. While purifying the divination area will help, peace of mind and calmness is not easy, particularly for the client who may well be distressed before they have a reading. Sometimes I have to lighten the mood, or talk about other things before the reading can take place. If the client still looks too serious, I will say something on the lines of "If you worry, I will start to worry, then you really will have something to worry about...!" This usually works. Bizarrely, those who walk in with the worries of the world on their face usually have little to worry about, while those who have a big smile and look happy are very often dealing with terrible situations in their life.

All good magicians observe the process of ritual to see which actions worked, and which actions failed or did not work as anticipated, which gives extra clues to the perceptive as to what may be going on in the life of the Querent, and it gives insight to the Reader as to how to improve instructions or presentation of the reading.

A Quiet Word about Fees

Fees are something tarot readers often feel uncomfortable about. If I did not charge for readings, I would starve or worse have to do some boring job in an office. The fee I charge is as much for my experience and knowledge as what I impart to the client. Being paid means that I am available for readings, and with recompense I am able to give more freely of my time and knowledge. From another point of view, I am giving what is important to me – knowledge, while I receive what is important to the client – money. All things are relative; I would rather give a discount to someone who is earnest but poor than negotiate with a wealthy client who wanted to pay less, thinking they are doing me a favour. The bottom line is that when I receive goods and services free of charge, I will do free readings!

Shuffling the cards

Card shuffling is better than the "Casino Riffle", but having said that, I have struggled to do a reading with cards that have been shuffled really well, and I have sailed through a reading where the client has given the most cursory of shuffles. Every so often I will get a client who will spread the cards over the table and give them a thorough rearranging, particularly reversing the cards. Where time is paramount, this is not usually a good idea though. Observing how the client shuffles the cards can give clues to the reading. Shuffling puts energy into the cards, which is a magical operation – energy is the capacity to do work. Occasionally, a card will fall out, and depending on my mood, I will take a look at it. Sometimes this card gives hints to the reading. Cards that fly out across the room onto the floor can suggest greater disruption in the life of querent, who really needs to get something out of their life – those cards need to be put back into the deck and shuffled together before continuing to the next stage. Throwing cards on the floor is not a good idea. Some clients have the knack of sticking the cards together, either during the shuffling or when they try to cut – this is a good indication that their life is stuck, a bit like constipation. If you see that the deck seems to be glued together, before they are cut, take the deck and loosen it up a bit. You may also see clients close their eyes and concentrate while shuffling. I am not so sure this is a good idea, as I want to see the bigger picture rather than the possibly narrow view the client desires to impose.

Cutting the Cards

The ritual of cutting the cards into four piles mirrors the magical actions of the Hegelian Dialectic, and care should be taken that the card cutting is performed correctly. Members of the Golden Dawn would know to cut the cards precisely in half each time, but most querents will not be party to this knowledge. I used to say "Please cut the cards in half, and place them to the right", but I quickly learned that for some reason in this situation people are incapable of knowing their rights from their lefts. Now, I make sure they position the deck of 78 cards to their left, my right, and then I ask the querent to "please cut the cards in half to there…" and I will point to where I want them placed, with enough space between the cut cards to place another pile. Some clients don't even listen to this, and they will plonk them down anywhere, or even attempt to restack the cards.

Since the ritual of shuffling and cutting the cards is the only active part played by the querent, and the ritual is designed to impose some kind of harmony between the inner and the outer, this inability to follow simple instructions suggests that the client is not listening to their own Inner Voice or intuition. Either way, the querent needs to be gently brought back to the proper method. Despite asking for the cards to be cut in half, they can end up at one extreme or another. If there seems to be less than say a dozen cards in one pile, it is a good idea to get the querent to cut the cards again, explaining that cards have to be cut into a total of four piles.

Despite the precision required by the Golden Dawn instructions, 78 is not divisible by four, so we are asking the impossible to start with. Some variation in the height of the four piles is desirable, since before they are turned over to reveal the top cards, the reader can see imbalances in the life of the querent. Fewer cards in the Water pile suggests low expectations in love, while an excess in the

Air pile shows many worries. A dominant Earth pile shows the client to be overly concerned with the outcome of events, while too many Fire cards can mean the querent is living in the past. Sometimes two of the piles are small, and the other two excessive, so there are other combinations to be considered.

Once the cards have been cut into four piles and turned over, the reader should be able to give an overview of the situation by looking at the elemental mix, elemental strengths and weaknesses, etc of the top cards, which may have to be balanced with the relative sizes of the four piles.

Beginning the reading

At the beginning of the reading, many querents will have indicated the nature of their problems. Having some kind of dialogue right from the start of the reading is important. The old fashioned method involves the querent sitting poker faced while the reader says his or her piece. There are many problems with this style. I have spent 20 minutes or more speaking at length without interruption, only for the querent to say they haven't understood what I am talking about, or what I said was not relevant. This is an incredible waste of not only my time but also the time of the querent and is very irritating, to say the least.

Querents are not there to test the reader; they are there to learn something about what is going on in their life. If I am barking up the wrong tree, I want to be told, and if I cannot say anything of relevance to the querent, I would rather terminate the reading there and then and return the fee.

Looking at things from another perspective, I appreciate the querent asking me to expand on a comment I made, or explore a particular avenue, as it means that they are getting a better reading. Just like every other person, tarot readers need feedback!

Another problem with old style readings is that they are delivered in the passive tense: "this will happen, that will happen, this person will do this…", the whole reading is conducted in a fatalistic manner, while my philosophy is that anything can be changed, and that the querent can change his or her life. I have had querents who have stated at the start of a reading that there is nothing whatsoever that they can do, and have no expectations of me finding something different. I always find at least one thing that can be done, which can be quite revelatory to the querent, changing how they see the situation.

Part of this process involves looking at the supposed intransigent situation from different points of view. A good reading should empower not only the querent but the reader too. If, for some reason, I do not understand quite why the querent is having a reading, I take a few minutes to clarify what the querent wants from me.

Determining which pile to read

This is something that is gained by experience. One method is to assign a Significator card, which in theory can be any of the cards. The Reader searches through the piles to find the card, being careful not to disturb the order of the cards. Once found, that pile is fanned out from left to right, so the top card is on the right.

If you have followed the previous chapters, the next stages should be familiar to you:

1. Elemental mix, groups of cards, reversals, etc.
2. Analysing the cards around the Significator, using Elemental Dignities
3. Card Counting.
4. If the Significator is not a Court card, try counting in both directions
5. Count from the top card
6. Count from any Court that seems significant in the context of the reading
7. Count from any card that represents any other topic that arises.
8. Card pairing
9. Unaspected Cards
10. Summarise the reading.

With experience you will no doubt find short cuts, methods that seem to work with particular clients and not at all with other clients. You may find that counting from the top card is all that is required. Be alive to the responses of the client, who may be curious about one of the cards in the sequence, so try counting and pairing from it. Many times when the client is talking about a situation it is as if the client is interpreting the cards, as I mentally card count through them.

The original Golden Dawn instructions specified reading only one of the piles, but feel free to read and interpret all four piles as and when necessary. There are good reasons for this. Sometimes I have found that reading all four piles gives a remarkably similar interpretation of events, which gives confidence. There are also occasions where the line of questions changes significantly, and it is necessary to change piles to interpret a particular significator. Where the reading gets particularly difficult, speaking in the third person can help – "The cards say…"

Another method is to announce a reshuffle of the cards and allow them to show the best way out of a situation, and then leave the client to make his or her own conclusions. Many clients are at crossroads in their lives, and they mistrust not only the advice of people around them, but also their own inner counsel. If possible, find ways of helping them to bring that confidence back. Do avoid those hackneyed clichés such as "meeting tall dark strangers" or "being at crossroads" or "travel over water". When a querent is looking for a new partner, talk less about how the new person may look, and more about where they might meet that person – put the querent in charge of their life.

You may be clutching at straws by the end of the reading, but do try to find something positive and uplifting to say as the client leaves – it could be the only thing they remember.

Having said all this, here is my version of the mechanics of a perfect reading – for client and reader alike.

The Perfect Reading...

The office is set up in a desirable location, the place has been purified, décor selected, consideration has been put into the layout of the waiting room and office. Advertising has started, business cards and any flyers produced. Clients will either be by appointment or they walk in off the street. After the fee has been paid, the reader endeavours to settle the client – those that are very keen can be just as difficult as those that are nervous. At this point it is a good idea to ask if the client has had readings before – newcomers may need some reassurance or clarification of what will be happening.

Hopefully the client will indicate any problem areas or the type of reading they require (the Opening of the Key Spread can handle pretty much anything – it depends on how the reading is approached), and some will say that they want to hear the good and the bad – nothing left out. Many clients are fearful of hearing bad news, but I point that the definition of bad news is entirely relative. Some clients come to a reading utterly clueless as to where they are going in life. This is a real challenge, and the best way to approach this is to get them doing something that boosts confidence, particularly if it involves education.

Once the cards are shuffled and cut into four piles, the Reader turns the piles over and interprets the top cards. On the basis of this interpretation, one or more of the piles will be fanned out and interpreted looking at the overall picture, then one or more cards will be counted and paired. Since the reading is a dynamic process, the client will be encouraged to comment or suggest avenues that can be explored. Some Querents have already decided on the direction they wish their life to take, and they are using the reading to confirm this. This is most illuminating for the client, who may see that the direction they intended to go may not be the best method of getting from A to B.

My regular clients will often spend the first five or even ten minutes telling me what has been going on since the last reading, and then they will tell me what they have actually come about. This is the smart way to get the most of out of a Tarot reading. I always point out that nothing is fixed – everything can be changed (whether it is worth changing some things in one's life is another question). If possible, give alternative methods for achieving the goals desired by the Querent, so they have more choice in their own destiny, show them that fatalism is not a good idea. End the reading if possible with saying something inspiring or comforting about the situation, and make an appointment for another reading.

Predictions

Making predictions is easy and accurate using The Opening of the Key Spread. When making timings, we ignore both Elemental Dignity rules and divinatory meanings and look at the astrological attributions of the cards. Depending on the circumstances (and there are times when vagueness is desirable), we have a number of different time frames that can be used. We can predict an event to happen to the month, day, or even hour.

The twelve major arcana attributed to the Signs of the Zodiac can indicate the time of the year the particular sign covers

The seven major arcana attributed to the planets can indicate the day of the week of that planet (ie: Sun=Sunday, Moon=Monday, Mars=Tuesday etc.)

Each of the minor arcana from 2 to 9 are associated with a decanate (ten day period) of the Zodiac. If necessary, events can be tied to these times.

My tarot readings are usually for the next six months in the future, so I look for Tarot cards that represent periods within that time. If am doing a reading in September, and the Death card is prominent, I would say that "the event happens from the end of October to the middle of November" (23rd October – 22nd November being the period ruled by Scorpio assigned to the Death Card). The client will be impressed, and with any luck, none the wiser as to how I made the prediction.

For greater accuracy, I look at ten-day periods. It just so happens that the 6 Cups is also prominent, so I could say that the event happens from around November 3rd to November 13th (the 6 Cups is assigned to the 2nd decanate of Scorpio which covers this period).

When events are happening in the next week, it is possible to predict the actual day simply by looking for planetary Major cards, so if the reading is done on a Monday, the appearance of the Empress card (Venus) would indicate Friday, the 'day' of Venus.

What will happen on a particular day?

Occasionally, the querent will want to know what will happen on a particular day. How do we assign cards for this, and how would we interpret them? Say the client wanted to know what would happen on the 24th June 2003. At this time, the Sun is in Cancer (Chariot) or the first decanate of Cancer, Two of Cups, and it is a Tuesday, ruled by Mars, Tower. Using the Opening of the Key spread, we would look at the top cards to see the overview, then we would look through the four piles to see the where the three cards are positioned, and see if they have a relationship either by Counting or Pairing. If the Tower card is in a different pile to the Chariot or Two of Cups, it is quite possible that the expected event does not happen. We would not use Elemental Dignities to understand the relationship between the three cards, particularly in this case since Fire and Water are enemies, but we would look at the Elemental Dignities of the cards surrounding them.

Fuzzy Periods

The Aces and Princesses do not have astrological attributions, but we can still assign time periods for them. The Princesses rule the seasons, while the Aces represent the four quarters of the lunar cycle. The three Major Cards Fool, Hanged Man, and Judgement/Aeon traditionally do not have astrological attributions, but many tarot readers assign the outer planets Uranus, Neptune and Pluto respectively. Since all these planets move very slowly, we can ignore them for predictive purposes. If circumstances dictate it, we can use these cards as indicating that it isn't possible to accurately predict events, which can be something of a relief to the querent.

Looking at the past

Very often when doing a reading, we are discussing events that have happened in the past, and it is possible to tell the client when the event happened by looking at the Major sun-sign cards to see if any can suggest a time frame in the previous six months. In my example above, if I am doing the reading in September, and the Lovers (Gemini) card is prominent in the past positions, I could suggest that the event happened in June (the month covered by Gemini). In these circumstances, it is not necessary to look for a relationship or choice that had to be made then. Another way round is to ask if something special happened in June that relates to why the client is having a reading. The client will be so surprised that they offer extra information that could clarify the reading.

CHAPTER NINE

Justice (Adjustment), Death and the Nines

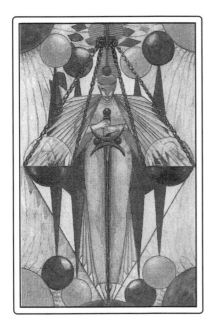

Justice or Adjustment = 30, Lamed
Air, Libra, Single Letter

Death = 50, Nun
Water, Scorpio, Single Letter

80 in gematria has meanings for KLL universal, general, KS Throne, OY town ruins, SK crowd, VOD union, assembling, YH ADNY God of Yesod and Malkuth, and YSVD Yesod.

The previous two pairings prepared us for the wedding that is promised in the Lovers and Art cards. The contract has been delivered in Adjustment. The Shekinah in Malkuth has been elevated to the Throne of Binah, the Mother. Libra, the sign allied with this card, is also the 7th house, which as well as ruling legal contracts and legal relationships, also signifies the world at large, hence SK crowd, VOD union, assembling.

Crowley is not entirely honest when he says that the secret keys of the Book of Law have not been published, since much of the Book of Thoth is devoted to the subject. He lifts part of the veil by hinting that part of the answer is found in the Fool and Adjustment, whose letters form AL, the name of the Book of the Law, and a Name of God. LA means 'not', in other words, everything that is not God. The first letter Aleph is composed of ALP. The final letter Peh is related to the Tower, and when we read Crowley's commentary on the Tower card, where he says, "… magical symbols must always be understood in a double sense, each contradictory of the other," we are back to the Hegelian Dialectic.

By uniting opposites, we create something new. The "Vision and the Voice" is quoted in the Fool commentary: "For below the Abyss, contradiction is division; but above the Abyss, contradiction is Unity". The annihilation of opposites elevates one to a higher position. The great advantage of this powerful magical technique is that very little energy is required of the magician. Towards the end of the commentary, Crowley says: "She represents Manifestation, which may always be cancelled out by equilibration of opposites."

The Death card is more complex than many commentators suggest. Crowley commences his analysis of the card with the words "… the letter Nun, which means a fish: the symbol of life beneath the waters." He sees alchemical putrefaction as a series of changes, which results in the Orphic egg, another symbol of life. As Kether is in Malkuth, life is within death. Death is the rhythm of life. The primary symbols of this card are the Eagle, the Serpent, and the Scorpion, which are united in the Dragon (see Liber Aleph, Chapter 157).

Yesod

The gematria value of Yesod is also 80, which is in itself justification for transposing Justice and Lust in order to get this gematria values. The straight line from Tipareth balances, compensating for the weak unbalanced energies from Hod and Netzach. Yesod is the Foundation of the Universe; it represents stability, yet the planet associated with Yesod is the Moon, a symbol of flux and change. We can see Yesod as transmitting the energies from the Tree via the Moon in all its various phases, to Malkuth. Yesod is watery, receptive, so the gathering of these forces is passive, just as the Moon is illumined by the Sun.

The sexual organs are located at Yesod, so it is appropriate that the paired Major cards are Justice and Death. The value for Lamed 30 and Nun 50 is 80, which has meanings for KLL universal, general, which shows pervasiveness of this sephirah; KS throne a symbol of Binah; OY town, ruins, possibly referring to the destructive nature of Death, while VOD, union, is suggestive of the sexual nature of Yesod as it represents the genitals.

The Nines

Three nines show added responsibilities, while four nines indicate much correspondence.

9 Wands – Lord of Strength

Balance is maintained by change and stability. The Moon is weak in Sagittarius, but since both fluctuate, their mobility is Strength.

9 Cups – Lord of Happiness

Jupiter rules Pisces which is doubly lucky, but the full satisfaction will run out in the end. There is no permanence in this situation, so enjoy it while it lasts.

9 Swords – Lord of Cruelty

Mars in Gemini is agony in the mind. Thinking and analysis is undermined by the realisation that nothing will go anywhere.

9 Disks – Lord of Gain

The only consideration is gain; profits are all that matters.

The Visionary Experiences of the Shaman

Not everybody is comfortable with ritual magic, the Golden Dawn or the O.T.O.. Shamanism is a system based upon the four elements, and has been around for thousands of years. The author has always had a synthetic approach to magic and spiritual development, incorporating aspects from ritual magic, shamanism, the tarot and Kabbalah. A pragmatic approach wins over doctrine – in the end it is what works that counts.

The definition of shamanism is varied, but the importance of shamanic work within a community cannot be over-emphasised. Mircea Eliade defined it as a Technique of Ecstasy. Magicians are not shamans, but shamans can be magicians.

The shaman uses altered levels of consciousness or trance that enables him to travel through the spiritual realms in order to perform actions to benefit the community. Shamans are able to communicate and command spirits; rarely will a shaman allow himself to be possessed by spirits. 'Shaman' is a Siberian word, but shamanic experiences have been recorded throughout the world.

Religious experiences in Siberia include a Great God or Creator, whose name often means Sky or Heaven, or having the characteristics of luminosity or loftiness. White Light or Master of the Sky is another epithet. This God has several 'Sons' or 'Messengers' subordinate to him who live in the lower heavens. Their number is usually seven or nine. These Messengers watch over and help human, and shamans are the link between the two. Later, as knowledge and power degraded, there appear to be division between the Messengers.

Finding the Shamanic Vocation

The shamanic life often begins with a spiritual crisis or 'separation'. Either hereditary transmission or spontaneous calling recruits shamans. Traditionally, those who become shamans by their own free will are not as powerful as those who are recruited and trained. The training is carried out by two methods; ecstatic (dreams, trances etc), or traditional.

Whether or not shamanism is hereditary, signs of potential ability from puberty include: nervousness, desire for solitude, being absent-minded or dreamy, even epileptic fits. Many latent candidates sleep excessively. A spirit in a dream of his vocation may instruct the person. However, the person still has to prove to the spirits of his abilities through various tests. In other words, the process may take some years before the person is accepted as a shaman within the community.

The spirits give the initiate prophetic dreams, or carry him to the underworld in order to be instructed by deceased shamans. Someone going through this process may exhibit sudden changes in moods; from irritability to normality, or melancholia to agitation, for example. The prospective shaman may try to extend his powers more as a mean of personal survival, but this result in abilities to protect society at large.

Symptoms of shamanism may be similar to mental disorder, and care has to be taken, but the shaman is considered to be one who has cured himself of all his maladies. In other words, the vocation of the shaman is to cure his own illness. For some shamans, perfect health is attainable only as long as shamanism is practised. Shamans are often very intelligent; they have a supple body and unbounded energy. In some cultures, the shamanic vocabulary is three times that of the tribe. We may consider that because they were ill, and then cured themselves, shamans have the theory and practise of illness and its cure.

The experience of dreams and ecstasies is the signal for the elder shamans to begin teaching the student. The main structure to an initiation is of suffering, death, and resurrection.

Initiations follow this general pattern:

- Dismemberment of the body
- Renewal of the internal organs
- Ascent to the sky and dialogue with the gods and spirits
- Descent to the underworld and dialogue with spirits and souls of dead shamans
- Visionary revelations.

The process of the emergent shaman is characterised by him becoming meditative, seeking solitude, sleeping a great deal, appearing absent minded, and having prophetic dreams.

Some traditions maintain that each shaman has an eagle or mythological bird that cuts the shaman's body in pieces and gives them to the evil spirits to eat, which gives the shaman the power to control disease in the future. Once the spirits depart the bird re-assembles the body. We can consider that the body parts have either been 'cleaned' or replaced. The eagle lives in a great tree, where she lays her eggs depends on the quality of the shaman.

Other shamans 'travel' across deserts or ascend a mountain where they enter a cave. The initiating shaman or spirits then cut up the bodies and cook them in a giant cauldron. Then, either the waters or a blacksmith reassembles the body. Some shamans experience torture by the demons (who are actually shamans). The shamanic experience is often undergone by the initiate sleeping in a graveyard or on the grave of a saint. In some cultures, quartz or a piece of bone, or other item is placed within the body of the shaman when his body is reassembled.

Enlightenment follows, which the initiate experiences as a luminous light (inner light) within his body, which enables him to see in the dark, perceive the future or hidden events, and the secrets of others. The experience is often in terms of height or depth, ascending a tree or flying as a bird. In Tantric, Buddhist or Christian traditions the initiate contemplates or visualises himself as a skeleton. To summarise, the shaman's body is dismembered and reassembled using fire (cooking).

Shamanic Powers in the Past

Historically shamans were capable of physically flying through the air. Interestingly, the origin of the first shaman is associated with the outbreak of evil, either in society, or that the shaman was too proud to recognise God. God had to intervene in the form of an eagle. The result was that 'good' and 'evil' shamans were created. In the beginning, initiatory death and resurrection was the criteria for creating a shaman, not teaching by spirits and elder shamans.

Spirits

There is a big difference between the spirit that chooses the shaman, and the assistant spirits who are subordinate to the shaman. There may be strong sexual elements involved in the development of shamanic powers. In dreams or visions there may be sexual intercourse between a spirit and the shaman, and it is this that transmits the power. There are also many stories of ordinary people having sexual relations with spirits.

Shamans often meet, or are initiated by souls of dead shamans. The ability to see spirits, whether awake or in dreams is a sign of shamanic ability. The ability to see the dead implies that the shaman is dead to the world too, which is why he has to undergo the dismemberment and resurrection process described above. It may be that the dead soul 'possesses' the shaman, and the experience is of soreness within the body. The souls of the dead act as a guide to the shaman when he travels in spirit through the cosmic regions.

The vision of spirits actually seems to equate with magical power and they appear in frightening forms; humans with animal heads recall the 72 Goetic spirits, or the Godforms of Ancient Egypt. If one experiences such a spirit, it is vital that no fear is shown, for the perception of them implies power over them and in fact they will become helpers. Spirits can appear in animal form when they assist on shamanic journeys. In today's technological age it is quite possible that spirits are more likely to have an AK47 than a sword or spear.

Spirits appear to a talented shaman without any effort, but for other shamans work is required. The shaman does not pray or make sacrifices to his spirits, but he can suffer if the spirits are displeased. Because the shaman is already 'dead', he can transform himself or identify himself with his spirits. This can also be taken to mean that he is able to unite or return to nature. In other words, the shaman becomes spirit in order to travel to other realms.

Secret Language

Shamans learn a secret language to communicate with spirits. The language can represent the sounds of animals. The shaman knows the language of nature, and as such, he has the freedom to travel throughout the worlds. The shaman has to be initiated by an animal, often a tiger or eagle to learn the language. The initiation can happen in dreams or the animals may be physically real. Physical pain can be a sign of spiritual initiation, and the pain or ache can actually have a personality or even move around the body.

Healing

The cause of illness is considered to be the theft or rape of the soul. The shaman has to capture the lost soul and force it back to the patient. In other cases the patient is possessed by an evil spirit, or a magical object has been placed in the body - sometimes is a combination of the two. The shaman has to remove the cause. There is a common root in that it is a requirement of the shaman to return things to their original state. Only a shaman can undertake this work as he has already been through these experiences. From this perspective shamans are infinitely more qualified to treat disease - how many western doctors have experienced the diseases they treat?

The resourcefulness and bravery of the shaman is quite remarkable as he makes his healing journeys. The shaman has to discover the cause of the illness; the spirit, its type and place in the hierarchy in the universe, who caused the spirit (another shaman, or self-inflicted), and how strong the spirit is. The shaman's spirits are sent out to find out the situation, and then the shaman has to fight it himself, which can often mean taking the spirit within himself, and therefore suffer just as much if not more than the patient. The denouement is usually ascension into the heavens to negotiate with the guardian spirits.

Danger is present at all levels. Some shamans are able to suck or pull objects out of the body. They may even appear to perform an operation complete with blood. These objects are usually thrown into water to neutralise them, or be carried off by spirits. However the shaman heals for the individual or society, he is bringing the universe back into equilibrium.

Cosmology

There are three levels: Sky, Earth and Underworld, connected by a central axis. The shaman uses the axis to communicate or move through the worlds. Some spirits or gods are able to use this axis as well, but usually only shamans or holy men can do it. There is a Centre or Sacred Space, which can actually be within the shaman. Pillars that reach up to the Pole Star represent the axis. At the basis is a stone altar. A snake is often associated with the pillar. Other symbols are a mountain, pyramid, temple, royal city, tree, bridge, stair or ladder. These symbols are cosmological or universal, while personal or microcosmic experiences are of a tent or house with a hole in the roof, so that everyone is connected to a universal centre.

Visions of a personal house can be very revealing to a shaman: a man living in a small house may actually believe he is in a mansion, or his workplace may be seen. In other words, the distortions and expansions between reality and the inner man reveal much about how he actually sees himself. Comparing the ability of the shaman to visualise his own awareness as a world view of the cosmic mountain with his vision of other people's 'home' show an extraordinary ability. It is also worth noting that the symbolism is constant throughout the world as long as we take into account cultural differences. To put things simply, humans live in their homes, while shamans have the whole cosmos to reside in.

Trees are particularly strong metaphors: the branches reach to the heavens, the trunk connects to the earth, with the roots extending to the underworld. There are birds (divine beings) in its branches; the leaves, flowers and fruits symbolise humans or branches of knowledge, which is reflected below. The trunk is usually indivisible, which indicates that unity is actually only experienced on this level of earth, despite appearances to the contrary. Trees are symbols of life. One connection that may be considered is the magical staff or wand carried by a shaman (and, for that matter a magician).

Generating heat

One characteristic of shamans is the ability to control or create heat. Healers have the ability to generate heat in the hands or at the point of healing, but shamans can work with fire.

Vedic techniques

The Rig Veda includes many shamanic techniques: to call back a soul, the priest addresses the dying man: "Although thy spirit have gone far away to heaven or ... the four quartered earth, we bring back that (spirit) of thine to dwell there, to live long." Another prayer - "May thy spirit ... come back again to perform pious acts; to exercise strength; to live; and long to see the sun. May our progenitors, may the host of the gods, restore thy spirit; may we obtain for thee the aggregate of the functions of life". In other texts, the priest has to summon back various organs from the cosmic regions. The instability of the soul is known, and there are warnings not to wake the sleeper suddenly in case he loses his soul. The siddhis mentioned by Patanjali include the ability to leave the body at will, and even to enter the body of another. Knots, bonds and nets are used to capture spirits, and to cause black magic.

Other myths and symbols

Shamans sometimes meet a funerary dog when he descends to the underworld. Shamans can turn themselves into dogs or wolves. Shamans reach ecstasy by travelling through the air use horses. The horse is an image of death, so it enables the shaman to enter other worlds. The hobbyhorse is a reflection of this. Eight legged horses are common in shamanic myths, again connected to funerals. Blacksmiths and their wives are venerated. Smiths are masters of fire and transformations, and often initiate shamans. Blacksmiths are also able to construct chains used to imprison evil spirits. The beating of metals can be compared to the dismemberment of the shamanic body. Working of metals also indicates alchemical processes.

Bridges

Once, all people had easy access to the three worlds. Now dead souls and shamans have to cross a bridge in order to reach the underworld. Crossing bridges are dangerous - the impure will find the bridge reduced to a knife-edge, with many evil spirits waiting to pounce. Initiates cross easily. Some magical rites attempt to create or build a bridge or ladder, and there are parallels in Arthurian legend, Islamic and Christian religions, where the bridge is as narrow as hair, or a sword bridge. The person has to pass through a narrow space guarded by demons. In some cases the shaman is unable to get back.

Ladders

A common motif - Jacob's Ladder when he falls asleep on the sacred stone at the centre of the world; Mohammed sees a ladder rising from the temple in Jerusalem, with angels either side. Other cognate examples are seven rung ladders (Seven Heavens), columns of smoke, rope, sunbeams, or a rainbow. Sometimes an arrow is used to pull the initiate upwards.

Shamanic Techniques

Shamans and shamanic techniques are found in all cultures around the world. Ethnologists have managed to define five characteristics of shamanism:

- One who enters and leaves altered states of consciousness at will
- One who can travel through inner world in his altered state of consciousness.
- Journeys that are undertaken to obtain power and knowledge, and to help other people.
- The reality experienced by the shaman is different and hidden to others.
- In these different states of consciousness, the shaman interacts with power animals, teachers, spirits, demons, and spirits of the dead.

This list enables us to distinguish between shamans and others who practice spiritual techniques. For example: Priests do not travel in altered states of consciousness. Mediums contact spirits, but usually in the form of possession, and they generally do not journey. Mentally ill patients can interact with spirits, but usually as victims. Meditators enter altered states of consciousness but they do not journey. Those who do similar things to shamans are witches, sorcerers, magicians, etc. Historically, shamanism is essentially a rural activity, while magicians are usually urban based.

One activity of the shaman is to act as Psychopomp or guide persons recently dead in their journey to the spirit world. If there are problems or obstacles to this the shaman has techniques to fulfil his or her task. The shaman is often a healer for the community by removing spirit intrusions in the individual, or return things stolen. The shaman has spirit guides who are often in the form of animals, and these work for him - possibly this is the origin of the idea of witches familiars.

Shamans work through visions in a dynamic manner - they can change and manipulate consciousness. Shamans are not only able to forsee the future, but also to change the outcome. As an example, shamans can find out where food or game is located for the community or avert threats to the community. This is a vital difference between shamanism and clairvoyancy.

There are many techniques for entering altered states of consciousness - drugs, hallucinogens, and dancing or monotonous music. Traditionally, potential shamans exhibit behavioural patterns that mark them out for training by the local shaman. Experienced Shamans are able to enter and leave these states without any external aid.

Vital to the shamanic world is a structure within which the shaman can work and move. There are many variations, but central to all systems are the four directions and associated elements (Fire, Water, Air and Earth), with a vertical axis that is divided into three levels or worlds. At the centre there is either a Cosmic Tree or Mountain that is used to gain access to the worlds. There are many names and descriptions for these worlds, but a basic guide is:

World	*Inhabitants*
Upper	Guides and teacher, 'Gods'.
Middle	Confused, trapped, or destructive spirits. Dead humans, black magicians. Records of past lives and future trends.
Lower	Power animals, allies or familiars.

Psychologists have analysed drug-induced experiences, which parallel shamanic knowledge, and are worth mentioning in this context:

1   Feelings of cosmic unity and ecstasy.
2   Feelings of enormous and endless pain and suffering, hopelessness and
    engulfment.
3   Intensified pain and suffering, explosions, destruction by fire, torture,
    sacrifices, battles, sexual and sadomasochistic orgies, the experience of
    dying.
4   Feelings of rebirth and release.

These experiences are analogous to the passage through the birth canal, and
are thus initiatory. We are discussing visionary or internal experiences, and should
not be confused with activities found in some cults.

Power Animals

Power animals are archetypes of the species; therefore they are indestructible
and eternal. Power animals are wild; tame animals or pets have no real power.
Insects are generally symptoms of diseases. There are exceptions such as
scorpions, spiders and bees. Power animals who come to the shaman are generally
friendly. There is a reciprocal relationship between the shaman and the power
animal that is equal but in different dimensions. The shaman brings energy and
the experience of human life, while the animal brings power, protection and the
ability to perform actions more efficiently. Power animals fall into four main types
or elements, and this depends upon the direction they are called from:

Fire	Lions, tigers, wolves, panthers.
Earth	Bears, horses, apes, elephants
Water	Fish, whales, otters, seals, dolphins
Air	Eagles, falcons, hawks.

Access to inner worlds is usually through a gate, cave, spring, or the roots of a
tree. The entrance is found by an inner descent until a terrain is seen, which can
be countryside, jungle, desert or water. Nearby an animal should be found. The
animal may be in a distressed condition, so it may be necessary to give the animal
appropriate food and drink. If the animal is agreeable it will accompany or guide
the shaman through the landscape, possibly to lead to other animals that can help.
(Courses on Shamanism give the impression that finding just one power animal is
an incredible achievement, but my experience is that successful shamans have a
whole range of animals that assist them.)
    In the early stages it is vital that the shaman returns exactly the same route.
After a few practice runs, the animal can appear to the shaman during normal
states of consciousness if necessary, or if the shaman wills it.

Benefits of power animals include increase in luck and positive attitude, lack of depression and loneliness, and protection from accidents and illness. Some power animals can stay with a shaman for months or years, while others either change on a regular basis or take the shaman to another power animal. Change is a sign of progress. It is important that personal experiences with power animals are kept private in order to preserve power and strength, or the animal may leave.

Cosmic Models

The Qabalistic Tree of Life, with its many version and structures, is a very useful model for shamanic work. The purpose of using the Tree of Life is not only to explore cosmic realms, but also to create balance and order between polarities such as Male and Female, into wholeness. The technical term is Tikkun or Rectifications, where the highest points of the cosmos are united to the lowest (our physical world). The sephiroth on the Tree of Life can be considered to be archetypes of the elements, and thus can be explored using shapes or symbols:

Earth	Yellow square
Water	Silver crescent (tips up)
Air	Blue Circle
Fire	Red triangle
Akasha	Purple oval or egg shape

Tattwa (element) journeys are possibly by visualising the combination of two element symbols so that the shaman is able to walk through them as if by a gate. This journey can be done with a power animal (ensuring the elements are harmonious with the animal). First signs are of smoke or fog, which will disappear to reveal a scene. Symbols seen during the journey can be related to circumstances within the life of the shaman. Once complete, the journey should be ended by returning back the same way and closing the 'door'.

Other Gateways

In addition to the Tattwas or elements, we ascribe the planets to the sephiroth. Use can also be made of the 22 Tarot Trumps as astrological gateways to other worlds. One can also work through the Court Cards and Minor Cards, but it is probably better to visualise the Tarot in sum to maintain coherence and wholeness within the awareness. Otherwise, one would have to make 78 different journeys which few have the time and resources to achieve. Care should be taken not to commence such actions during adverse lunar tides. In addition to these exercises, it is advisable to practice the use of mantras or words of power from a spiritual tradition, but these are beyond the scope of this essay.

We now look at the structure or hierarchy of the Worlds, although notions of one being 'better' than another have to be abandoned. Balanced access to all worlds using the appropriate cosmic model over-rides favouring one method over another, or one particular level over another, which is reflected in the way the Tarot is approached in this book. In other words, the vision of 'reality' mirrors one's own level of psychic or spiritual development. In these circumstances it should be obvious that changes or developments in spiritual awareness will undoubtedly indicate changes in the model.

As a general guide, the Upper, Middle and Lower worlds can be characterised thus:

World	Experiences
Upper	Yang or masculine, active, intellectual, expansive, abstract. Pastel colours, floral smells.
Middle	Encountering evil. Processes of action and its consequences; past lives, the progress of departed humans and spirits, finding lost objects.
Lower	Yin, female, passive, concentrated, concrete, focused on feeling. Deeper, primary colours, earthy smells.

At each level there is also a directional aspect.

Invoking and Evoking

Invoking is a vertical procedure, bringing power down from higher levels. Evoking is horizontal, creating an artificial element to obtain knowledge, or produce changes in the world, or meet spirits from other worlds or universes. The danger of mediumship or channelling is like having an open house policy: anyone or anything is invited without discrimination. Spirits in this context are usually of a low quality, which rarely bring new or interesting knowledge.

The point or principle of shamanic work is to enhance the evolution not only of the shaman but the community he represents, rather than gain control of, or power over others. Wealth is unlikely to accrue. Unlike meditation techniques, where the emphasis is on quieting the mind and senses, shamans need high arousal, either through drums or monotonous sounds, or walking with the eyes unfocussed.

Chakras

There is a Golden Dawn technique named the Middle Pillar technique, which is basically a visualisation of the Tree of Life imposed around the body of the shaman, with the Middle Pillar centred through the body, the Crown sephira at or above the head, with Malkuth at or below the feet, surrounded by a brilliant white light. Advanced techniques involve visualising a column of Tree of Lifes above and below the shaman, with which he can ascend or descend.

Use of the will or unity of desire in a visualisation can create changes that will manifest in the material world. Spiritual practises should be performed in secrecy and in solitude, although there can be benefits in spiritual association with another shaman of like mind.

Sacrifice

Sacrifice is an important aspect of any magical act. *This means that we have to create space within the environment for the action or change to take place.* Unconscious desires will always subvert intention, so it is necessary to dissolve both the desire and it's opposite in order to create space. What is necessary is to destroy the polarity that exists, in order to create asymmetry. In other words, once the magical act has been performed, it is vital to forget everything and return to the normal waking state. Speculation about the possible results will weaken the process. The concentration is on the goal, not the process, or how it may occur. This is because it is up to the powers of nature who know far better how to fulfil the magic. Once achievement results it is also important that the gains are consolidated. We might get a million pounds, but we may also have the unwelcome interest of the tax man! We have to use the results of a magical action immediately, or the same processes that brought the manifestation will take it away.

Exploring the Cosmic Realms

Once the four directions have been created and maintained within the awareness of the shaman, a natural and dynamic balance of these elements is formed. A framework or structure is also created with the awareness of the shaman in which to work. With the horizontal components set up, the vertical aspect can be explored. For ascensions, we begin from a high point, atop a mountain for example, having set the directions. Alone, or with a power animal, fly up to the Upper World to find a teacher in human form. After seeing clouds and space, a membrane has to be passed. Above this there will be many levels. Look for a human - if there is none, keep going up. Once met, question the person to see if s/he is your teacher, ask for a name, verify it, and then seek advice.

The process is always to go to a teacher, never inviting them to come to the shaman. On many occasions it is advisable to check with a God/dess before embarking on a magical act. To do this:

1   Ascend to the Upper World, see the colours fade to pastels.

2   Ascend through the colours of the rainbow, starting with red through to indigo, and then into white light.

3   Merge or expand with the light, which will detach the ego from selfish desires.

4   The God or Goddess may be seen as gigantic figures. Ask for their assistance, share in their experiences, learn as much as is possible.

5   Ask the God or Goddess the results of the intended magical action. Answers will be either visual or silent verbal messages.

One can consider the God and Goddess as aspects of one's own higher self, which is why only respect not worship is necessary.

Healing

The shaman must be powerful (full of power) during healing practises, otherwise there is a danger of being invaded by the spirit that is being removed. A space needs to be created in order to place the spirit away from the patient. Healing is developed by repeated practice and working with power animals. Also a strong and clear mental map of the spiritual realms has been created.

Removing Spirit Intrusions

In spirit vision, a tunnel associated with the patient can be located in the Middle World. Parasitic intrusions are usually seen as large, repulsive insects, slimy snakes, or sludge. The shaman washes, sucks, or pulls out the spirit, and puts it in a neutralising medium, such as water. The power animal may help with the process.

Extracting intrusions means that energy has been removed from the patient. The original, lost energy has to be located and replaced within the patient, otherwise the intrusion can return. Dealing with the reason or cause of trauma may also be necessary, which could originate from a previous life. Since energy cannot be lost, merely misplaced, it follows that there could be place where all these lost pieces of energy are stored. The technique is as follows:

There is a golden hall full of millions of locked boxes, guarded by a gatekeeper, who may be asked for permission to enter to look for the lost energy. Once the box has been located (this should be an automatic process) and opened, the pieces may actually jump out, and it is possible that the shaman will see the cause of the loss of energy in the first place. The energy piece(s) may be perceived as a light, crystal, box or previous form of the patient. These pieces have to be taken back through the colours of the rainbow, starting with indigo through to red. This process should purify the pieces, and they are then blown back into the patient. If they pieces refuse to return, they have to be forced, unless advised otherwise by your spirits.

To summarise, remove the intrusions from the patient's tunnel. Locate the missing energy in the Hall, bring it back through the colours of the rainbow, and place back in the patient.

Reincarnation

Sometimes it is necessary to find the cause of suffering or problems within a previous life. Using power animals is the best way as animals often have access to missing information. Curiosity is not a good reason for doing this process, as some very traumatic experiences can result. One reason for doing regressions is in order to create a greater sense of wholeness within one's life, where reconciliation will create freedom for the operator. Past lives are located within the Middle World, so a journey through a horizontal tunnel or cave is necessary, with your power animal/s in attendance. The tunnel will glow with primary colours starting with red going through to purple, and finally white. Questions can be asked when one arrives at a previous life: what is my age? Where am I? What are my parent's names? My sex? Previous lives are not necessarily presented in chronological or sequential order, and only particular aspects may be emphasized. The best method is for the shaman to order the power animal to go to the life relevant to the problem at hand. It is usually fairly easy to move backwards and forwards within a life, to move to the moment of death and beyond. Once the work is done, return via the way you came. It is possible that some people who appear in a previous life may also be in this life, but within different relationships, or even different sexes.

One philosophical result of these processes is the realisation that we are everything else, or that we have been everyone else at some point. Apart from death, the other major cause of trauma is birth, so this may be explored as well.

Psychopomp

A vital function of shamanism is to be a guide or helper of the dead. Many people who die are not necessarily aware of where they have to go, and so they can become trapped in the Middle World for a variety of reasons. A human spirit sometimes needs the extra energy a shaman and power animal can provide in order to complete the journey.

To help the dead, enter into a tunnel with a power animal, or ask a guide to take you to where the deceased currently resides. Another method is to think oneself at the place of the deceased. At the place, tell the deceased that you are there to help them. A period of time may be necessary to prepare for the journey. When the time is right, there may be a white light, or the deceased may meet already departed relatives and friends. The shaman may also have to escort the deceased to a bridge, or to a ferryboat, or whatever symbolism is appropriate to the belief system of the deceased. Crossing over with the deceased is obviously not a good thing, even if permitted.

Those who suffered from a violent death may be found trapped in a region, which has no colour, only black and white. The introduction of colour will assist the deceased, and it is possible that this action will aid others trapped there. There can also be a problem with faulty ideas and conceptions of what Heaven is actually like, so some people think they have arrived when of course it is an illusion.

Shamanism and Tarot

Shamanism involves travel in Spirit to a place to perform some kind of healing. We can consider the type of cards – Major, Minor, and Court, to show spiritual levels.

Tarot	*World*	*Inhabitants*
Major Arcana	Upper	Guides and teacher, 'Gods'.
Court Cards	Middle	Confused, trapped, or destructive spirits. Dead humans, black magicians. Records of past lives and future trends.
Minor Arcana	Lower	Power animals, allies or familiars.

Where all four cards are of one type, it is easy to know at what level to work, however, knowledge of probability shows that getting all Major or all Court Cards on the top piles to be fairly unlikely. Also, common sense needs to be applied, so an assessment of **all** four Strings and pointed questions to the Querent would be the minimum before considering Shamanic action.

If I see four Major cards, I would know that the Querent is acting in a fatalistic manner, so rather than resorting to supplication to a God, injecting a more positive attitude to life would be more useful. Similarly, four court cards on the top of the Strings is more likely to indicate that the Querent is being dominated by people around, or is listening too much to the views of others, or is overly concerned with what other people think. The 'plots' in Soap Operas revolve around people interfering in the lives of others, making a mess of it in the process, causing misery. Murder rates in soap operas are higher than average.

Conversely, having all four Minor Cards is generally positive, showing that the Querent is in control of the situation. Having all three types present may show a vertical ascent, but of course that would infer having the Major card on the Fire position, Court card on Water or Air, and a Minor card on the Earth position. Generally, Shamanic travel involves a journey to the Underworld to meet power animals, which accompany the Shaman on the journey elsewhere or in a particular direction.

There are several attributions of the elements to directions. My preferred method is the Polar Order where the directions balance the inimical elements, which the Golden Dawn attributions do not.

The top four cards can be re-ordered as follows:

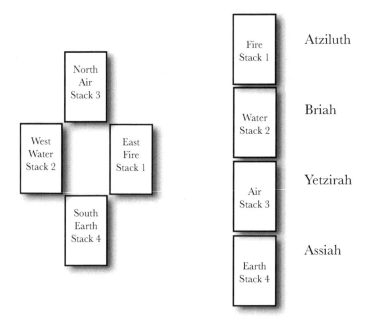

Each element has two aspects present, easy to see in the diagram above, which of course resembles the Celtic Cross Spread.

An excess of a particular element will show a bias in a particular direction or level of creation, while the absence of an element shows a similar lack of functioning. During a divination, the client will sometimes ask in what direction a person or event is likely to happen, so the attributions of elements to directions will be of assistance.

Magic , Shamanic Travel and the Celtic Cross

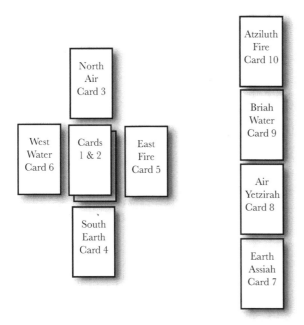

Cards 3 to 6 show a horizontal arrangement, while cards 7 to 10 are vertical, which suggests that the Celtic Cross spread is a two dimensional plan of a three dimensional world. This concept can be taken even further: cards 1 and 2 can be the top and bottom of the Cosmic Cube, and cards 3 to 6 are the four sides. Note also the order of the vertical cards - the YHVH order is the same as for the first stage of Opening of the Key.

Looked at this way, the Celtic Cross opens up many new avenues of research. For a start, the spread becomes a symbolic representation of a Shamanic Journey, which has huge potential for Magical travel and change.

Shamanic journeys involve travel from one place to another; therefore we can use positions 1 and 2 to our advantage. Card 1 is the elemental starting position, and Card 2 is the elemental finishing position.

The Shaman/Magician can travel either from a level corresponding to the column, or move in a compass direction, according to the nature of the operation envisaged. Put another way, if the first card is Water, we could either start in a western direction, or perform the actions at the Briatic level. Alternatively, we could see Card 2 as an elemental aspect of Card 1 in a similar manner to the elemental attributions of the Court Cards.

CHAPTER TEN

The Hermit, The Hanged Man, the Tens and the Princesses

The Hermit = 10, Yod
Earth, Virgo, Single Letter

The Hanged Man = 40, Mem
Water, Mother Letter

50 is the number of Nun, Death in the Tarot. Other meanings are: ADMH earth of Chesed, ATM closed, shut up, AYZBL Jezebel, ChBLY pains, sorrows, DG GDVL Jonah's whale, HMH to ferment, KL all, every, TMA unclean, impure, YM sea, MY, water, liquid, danger.

Jezebel is a notorious woman in the bible, responsible for the introduction of Baal worship, and for killing prophets, however, since the prophets were constantly exhorting the Jews to worship the One True God, we can safely assume the Jewish people were easily mislead, and there has been a consistent propaganda campaign against the woman. The combination of the symbolism of the Hanged Man and the Hermit can be seen in Jezebel.

The Hermit is equated with Virgo, ruled by Mercury, and the letter Yod, which is the first letter of Tetragrammaton, which immediately places the Hermit as Creator, and the Logos. In Gnostic terms, Creation is descent into matter, a source of evil, so there is some ambivalence concerning this card. As usual in the Book of Thoth, this card is intimately connected with the Supernal Triangle, but in this case it is the sperm in the womb of Binah.

Whereas the Hermit represents the Fire of YHVH, even though we think of him as earthy Virgo, the Hanged Man is Water, and it is a baptism of death (paradoxically, Crowley portrays the Death card as life). The Gematria values for the combination of Hermit and Hanged Man are most apt for the latter card. Both cards deal with the dark side of life.

DG GDVL, or great fish, is discussed in the Death card, where Crowley equates the fish with the serpent, and of course the fish is a symbol of Christ, and doctrines of resurrection or reincarnation, a recurring theme where the maiden becomes the woman.

The gematria references the 50 Gates of Understanding (Binah), a Kabbalistic term associated with the 50 Chapters of Genesis.

Malkuth

The magical image of Malkuth is of a young woman, crowned and throned. The crown is a symbol of Kether, while the throne is a symbol of Binah, so even though we are at the bottom of the Tree of Life, we are reminded not only that Malkuth is as Holy as the other Sephiroth, but Malkuth is at an equal level to Kether. Furthermore, the Sea is a symbol of Binah. In the *Book of Thoth*, the Princess of Disks, the last and therefore lowest card of the 78 is a *"woman on the brink of transformation"* as she is transformed from maiden to motherhood in Binah. The Hermit is related to Virgo, the Virgin maiden, and when the sun is in Virgo, we have harvest time. The pairing of the Hermit with the Hanged Man and Malkuth is evocative in the Book of Thoth, where a field of wheat appears in the Hermit card, and there is a wheat sheaf in the card of the Princess of Disks.

Malkuth is the place of the Goddess in Kabbalistic lore, but over the centuries much of this knowledge has been 'lost'. The transmutation of the maiden to the mother is found in Greek mythology, particularly Kore, Persephone and Demeter. Baal is the symbol of the Sun and is worshipped in "high places", and the Princess of Disks has a mountain in the background. Of course the highest is Kether, which also appears as a diamond, which is the precious stone associated with Kether.

The Tens

4 Tens indicate responsibility and worry, while 3 Tens show buying and selling

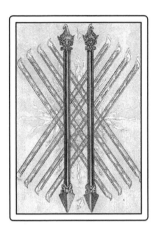

10 Wands – Oppression

The result of using dumb, blind force all the time results in tyranny.

10 Cups – Satiety

The realisation that when one achieves the goal, there is no feeling of satisfaction, but still one must pay.

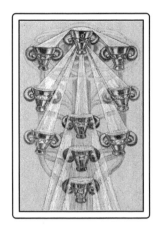

10 Swords – Ruin

If one keeps on fighting, all will end in destruction. However, there is hope – when the Governments have destroyed each other, there are still the peasants who will continue.

10 Disks – Wealth

When money accumulates beyond a certain point, its value becomes meaningless. Then, the use of the money has to change. The time to set up Charities or Foundations for the good of the population as arrived. The 10 Disks is the sum total of the Tarot cards, therefore it represents the fulfilment of the Great Work. When one achieves one's Holy Guardian Angel, the course of Magical and Spiritual Work will naturally change.

The Princesses

4 Princesses show new ideas or plans while 3 Princesses show groups of young people

Princess of the Shining Flame

She is the inexhaustible fuel of Fire, the impulse of Spring. To face her is to be consumed by her.

Princess of the Waters and Lotus of the Palace of the Floods

She is the power of crystallization, of manifestation, of creation, forever whirling about the North Pole.

Princess of the Rushing Winds. Lotus of the Palace of Air

From the creativity and benevolence of the Princess of the Waters, the pendulum swings to the vengeful and destructive powers of the Heavens.

Princess of the Echoing Hills. Rose of the Palace of Earth

The woman on the brink of transformation – to know her is to know the Heights and the Depths. She is the sign of attaining the Knowledge and Conversation of the Holy Guardian Angel.

Sex Magick

The Golden Dawn sex magical secrets were better kept than most, but it is clear that sex magick went on. Both Aleister Crowley and Dion Fortune were accused of publishing sex magick secrets inadvertently. In both cases neither knew what they had done until it had been pointed out to them.

Clearly sex magick is fundamental to spiritual and magical practice. Although Yesod represents the genitals, both male and female, the symbolism of the penis and vagina is found in the Supernal Sephiroth of Chokmah and Binah respectively. This is no accident. The highest levels of the Tree of Life are replete with sexual imagery, far more so than 'lower down'. The attribution of the Knight and Queen to Chokmah and Binah conveys more than authority, since these two figures are the parents of the Prince and Princess at Tipareth and Malkuth respectively. The clues to sex magick are contained therein since it is the union of opposites in Chokmah and Binah that cause creation further down the Tree, and not the bumping and grinding at Yesod. In other words, it is the collective visualisation of the sexual partners at the moment of orgasm that creates the thoughtform that may or may not manifest in the manner intended.

The reality for everyone is that **every** action is a magical action. How much more so for those working towards attainment of their Holy Guardian Angel! The result of every sex act is the creation of some kind of magical child, intended or not. The satiation of lust and the corresponding release of tension through orgasm is the foundation of sex magick whether it be heterosexual or homosexual, 'normal sex', masturbation, oral or anal.

The triangle is the primary symbol of sex magic since it unites the trinity. The union of opposites create a third force that has qualities of both opposites. Understanding of the Hegelian Dialectic is therefore fundamental to successful magical operations.

The union of Chokmah and Binah results in the 'false sephirah' Daath. Daath means knowledge, to know, the biblical euphemism for sex. Daath is considered to be the primary gate or entrance to other worlds or universes. We are all aware of how we can be transported somewhere else during sex, particularly the orgasm. However, sex magick is not a one-way street – there is up as well as down. The ascent of energies contributes towards spiritual emancipation and knowledge with one's Holy Guardian Angel. When both upward and downward motions are possible the triangle is transformed into the square, symbol of solidity, since an inverted triangle is a very unstable image. As well as the square we also have the cross, the crossing of spirit and matter, the essence of the Dialectic, which is how the aspirant can have union with God and survive, for to meet God is to become God. Since God is Transcendent, the aspirant will no longer exist!

In the Golden Dawn system, Malkuth is depicted as four quarters in the circle. As well as symbolising the unity of the four elements, it shows that above Kether is another Tree of Life where the closest point is Malkuth. The juxtaposition of Malkuth and Kether in this way creates two vortices like an hour glass. These vortices create the illusion of spinning – it is unclear which is stationary and which is moving. The illusion of movement is symbolised by the swastika, a development of the quartered circle, and illustrates dynamism within the normal static and stable square. If one wishes to know how to 'square the circle' I would suggest study here. The swastika is indeed the symbol of Kether, and is depicted in one of the sigils for Aleph in Liber 231.

In his book *Tarot and Magick*, Donald Michael Kraig suggests that 'tarot reader' should be replaced by 'tarot worker'. While the suggestion is admirable, the title is inelegant, sounding like some kind of socialism. Clearly the time has come to move away from passivity of Tarot reading to the dynamics of the Tarot cards within a reading. Ever since the discovery of Quantum Mechanics it is clear that the observer always has an influence on the reading. Here we have the dialectic of reader and client united in the obvious contemplation of the tarot cards, but since there is always the upwards direction, the possibility of creating a new reality for both is implicit. Kraig's book is clearly a milestone in the development of the Tarot as a magical solution to problems, but he did not have the information presented in this book. All the divinatory techniques of Counting, Pairing and Elemental Dignities are powerful magical techniques in themselves. While I have been aware of the power of Elemental Dignities as a magical technique it was only while I was working on the rather tedious recording of all the combination of the four strings of cards for this book that the magical power of Counting and Pairing revealed themselves, thus fulfilling the adage that like anything else worthwhile it is ninety percent perspiration and ten percent inspiration. Scattered throughout this book there are references to sex magick, some of which the author is not necessarily aware of, since the process of sex magick is to make the invisible visible.

Counting, Pairing and ED's all have the Hegelian Dialectic at their basis, which means that all three have sex magic at their basis. To use all three techniques at once in a tarot reading has an exponential effect. The power of magick in tarot is not the cards themselves but in the dynamics of the interchanges of energy that goes between the cards. The fundamental method of assessing Strings of cards is to build up the analysis between groups of three cards – the triangle. The outer cards 'create' the inner card, which already exists of course, and with the power of Elemental Dignities, an entirely new image of what is going on arises in the mind of the diviner. This image can be considered the 'Daath' solution, so we can surmise an alternative 'Kether' solution. If the client and reader are sufficiently spiritually aware, this avenue may be explored to some advantage.

Elemental Dignities are based upon the dialectic of opposites uniting to create a third force. Fundamentally we have Fire and Water creating either Air or Earth. Air and Earth are also mutually antagonistic, so we see a never-ending cycle, since in the kabbalistic system the Princess (Earth) becomes the Queen (Water) to start a new cycle of creation.

The Pairing of cards is another example of the Dialectic at work, except that the result is invisible, and this invisible link marks the beginning of the next pairing of the cards where the process is repeated. The Pairing of the Major cards for the purpose of creating a meditation had the unexpected result of creating a grimoire. The author had not expected to even attempt to explore this grimoire, but even so, the results were the partial exploration of Liber 231 in this book and the discovery of the Neophyte Spread.

Previously, I suggested that sex magick had the effect of making the invisible visible. Nowhere else is this exemplified in the Counting Technique. Without the extensive (and to be honest, boring) analysis of every single card in the tarot reading discussed in this book – the reader has been spared this experience since it was decided to include only the Fire String – the true nature of Unaspected cards would never have arisen. As a result of the discovery of the grimoire in the Paired cards and then finding the significance of the unaspected cards as the source of hidden spiritual power, and therefore the means for changing circumstances through magic, the spirits of Liber 231 made themselves known to the author – not only that, not to be outdone, the Goetic spirits also appeared. Since the Goetic spirits are relatively well documented, it has not been necessary to discuss them as much as the spirits of Liber 231 who are an unknown quantity. It is the author's contention that while entirely different, the Goetic spirits have equal status in the Tarot. The ramifications of such a situation pose fascinating possibilities that will have to wait for another book.

By now the reader must be under the impression that like the Victorians, the author sees sex everywhere! Certainly at one level this is true. Books on magic emphasise the importance of performing a divination before starting a magical operation. So here is a good opportunity to explore how Strings can be used for this purpose. My antipathy to the use of Significators is well known, but if the diviner assigns a court card Significator each for the partners in the proposed sex magick, the Strings can be analysed to see not only the compatibility, but the outcome for both partners, as well as the outcome for the act itself. Furthermore the timing and location of the act can also be explored. Clearly, the appearance of both Significators in the same String is a good sign, but what if the Counting reveals that neither Significator 'counts' onto the other? Does this signify failure? Perhaps, but maybe the Tarot is telling the magicians that masturbation, either separately or on each other is the preferred method rather than sexual intercourse. The arrangement of the cards in terms of dignity and whether upright or reversed can also give clues as to who will be the dominant partner. If one or more other court cards are present, they indicate other people who should participate, or that they represent people known or unknown who may be affected by the ritual. If there are only two significators, it is possible using the

Counting technique to determine who will be dominant. Clearly, there are many possibilities here that need careful analysis. Assuming that the prognostication is good for doing a ritual, the Tarot can provide not only the type of sex magic to be performed, but the magical power that will be exploited. The first stage is to count every card to identify all the Unaspected Cards. An Unaspected Minor Card would immediately suggest invocation of the associated Goetic Spirit. The power of an unaspected Major card depends on which pile it is found. Where there are several Unaspected Major cards, how they count onto to the Significator Court cards will determine the ritual.

If the magic is to be Ceremonial, the paired meditations of Liber 231 can be used in conjunction with the Neophyte Spread.

By now, the magician will know who is to participate and the purpose of the ritual, but not necessarily the method to attain the results. The sex-magical associations of the Major cards have been a closely guarded secret, but Kenneth Grant in Nightside of Eden gives the game away, appropriately in the chapter on Tempioth, the Qliphotic spirit of the Lust card. Before I do this, it is important to understand something of what Kenneth Grant is trying to do, at least as I understand it.

The primary purpose of the book *Nightside of Eden* is to discuss Kalas, a Tantric term which means time. There are 16 Kalas or powers, and Grant associates them with 16 types of vaginal secretions. Because there are two sides of the Tree of Life, we can double the number of Kalas to 32. This number is easier to deal with in Tarot terms since we can have powers associated with the ten Sephiroth and the 22 Major Arcana, and indeed the book is in two sections to reflect this. However, with Kenneth Grant nothing is simple. Here is his summary of the powers from the Introduction:

> *"The scheme that will be adopted here is based upon Liber CCXXXI which gives both the sigil and the name of the Beast that crawls along the twenty two paths, emitting as it goes the kalas and the bindus, and uniting the nectar of the woman with the venom of the Serpent.*
> *The twenty two paths of the Tree of Life transmit the influences of the eleven macrocosmic power-zones to their corresponding nerve-centres in the human organism. There are thus 33 kalas in all, 32 of which are of extra-terrestrial origin. Seven of them are cosmic power-zones, and the remaining three transmit extra-cosmic influences from the three forms of Nothing."*
> Kenneth Grant, *The Nightside of Eden*

Magical writing is not easy at the best of times, and Grant does his best to maintain a level of ambiguity, fulfilling the question mark as to whether there are ten or eleven Sephiroth on the Tree of Life. Mix in the eleven Grades of the O.T.O. and you have a heady mix. The 8th, 9th and 11th Grades of the Sovereign Sanctuary specifically relate to sex magick, and within them there are subdivisions. The 8th Grade involves masturbation, the 9th is coitus proper and the 11th 'comports the use of the lunar current, but others maintain that this grade involves homosexual sex. One meaning of the lunar current can be performing rituals during the waning moon.

The sophistication of Strings shows how complex magical rituals can be particularly useful when sex is involved. If the diviner was trying to discover if black magic has been used, it could be indicated by one or more cards being unaspected.

The Magical and Spiritual uses of the Tarot

Contemplate on the keys that I have given you here. With them, you can open many gates, sealed with many locks, since not everyone is worthy to enter through them.

Gates of Light

This book is intended not just for students of Tarot but for practicing magicians. While the reason for the first group is perfectly understandable, I can see magicians raising objections - why do they need to know Tarot? The few books on magic that mention Tarot, usually do so on the sensible grounds that it is a good idea to perform a divination to see if the desired results would be attained. The magical techniques I describe in this chapter require in depth knowledge of Tarot, the OOTK spread, the Kabbalah and sex magick. It is my belief, based upon many years study and work with the OOTK spread, that it was developed to be the practical application of the Sepher Yetsirah and the Bahir.

The Hermetic Order of the Golden Dawn has many magical techniques based upon the Kabbalah, but it is noticeable that there does not seem to be so much from the Sepher Yetsirah. They do include the Single, Double and Mother letters in their attributions of the Major Arcana, but the French schools had already done this. There is also mention of the Cosmic Cube which is also part of the Sepher Yetsirah, although this has never been adequately explained neither by the Golden Dawn nor by Kabbalists.

Within the description of the Opening of the Key Spread, however, there are enough clues, for those who know, to create a whole range of magical and kabbalistic techniques. For many years I have been using and studying the OOTK. On many occasions I have gained true insights or visions that are not directly

directly attributable to the divinatory meanings, and since I have not had formal study or training in the Golden Dawn system, it has been a struggle. However, I can now reveal some of the magical and spiritual techniques that can be developed using the Opening of the Key.

Tarot is something of a curate's egg. On the one hand it and the Opening of the Key spread stand at the apex of the Golden Dawn system, along with the Enochian Magical system, while on the other, the vast majority of books are rehashes of AE Waite's Rider-Waite deck that focus on the fortune telling aspects. To my mind, Tarot has advanced little in this respect. Let it be remembered that much of the esoteric knowledge of the tarot comes from Golden Dawn Adepti, and the Golden Dawn itself. In the Introduction to the Book of Thoth, Aleister Crowley makes it abundantly clear that the book is the product of his life's work that started with his initiation into the Golden Dawn. Crowley, for all his faults (and there are many) was probably one of the greatest magicians ever, so why did he persist with the Tarot? It cannot be for the fortune telling, as he made it clear in his letters that he did not want the Tarot to be used for this purpose.

Another great magician and contemporary of Crowley was Dion Fortune. She was a member of the Golden Dawn, and included many of their techniques into her own teachings. She admired in particular Crowley's work on the Thoth Tarot, he inscribed one of the earliest numbered copies of The Book of Thoth to her, and she visited Crowley at Netherwood near Hastings shortly before his death, to view the many rejected versions of the tarot cards along with the artist Frieda Harris. The importance both Fortune and Crowley placed upon the Tarot should give us clues that there is far more to the Tarot than we realise.

In order to see how the Opening of the Key spread can be used magically, it is necessary to look at the way the GD divided up the tarot cards for counting purposes, and analyse from a kabbalistic point of view.

The Court Cards

In the Opening of the Key spread, the King, Queen and Prince are attributed to YHVH, but of course they are three when YHVH has four letters. Why is this so? In the Introduction to The Kabbalah Unveiled, Mathers says:

> *"But this forgoing triple division of the soul is only applicable to the triple form of the intellectual, moral, and material. Let us not lose sight of the great qabalistical idea, that the trinity is always completed by and finds its realisation in the quaternary; that s, IHV completed and realized in IHVH – the trinity of:*

Crown	*King*	*Queen*
Father	*Son*	*Spirit*
Absolute	*Formation*	*Realisation*

"Completed by the quaternary of:

Absolute One	Father and Mother	Son	Bride
Macroposopus, the Vast Countenance	Father and Mother	Microprosopus, the Lesser Countenance	Malkuth, the Queen and Bride
Atziloth, Archetypal	Briah, Creative	Yetzirah, Formative	Asiah, Material

And to these four the soul answers in the following four forms: - Chiah to Atziloth; Neshamah to Briah; Ruach to Yetzirah; and Nepthesch to Asiah."

I have retained Mather's spelling of the Kabbalistic terms here. This quotation neatly encapsulates how one should view the Court cards, as indicating levels of creation within the Kabbalistic system. Some may feel that I have given too much away on this subject, so I will not elaborate, except to say that the placement of the court cards within the OOTK spread could indicate either imbalance within those levels, or which particular level the magician should work at.

The Aces

The Aces represent four elements plus spirit, which is why we count five. This is confirmation that the Aces are not concerned with the elements they represent, and why good books on Tarot describe the Aces as the 'Roots of the Powers of the Elements". Aces as Kether represent the Point, and in essence they do not act. One might also consider the Pentagram, but at a more exalted level than the Pentagrams are usually considered.

The Mother Letters

Aleph, Mem and Shin are the Mother Letters, and the Sepher Yetsirah goes to considerable lengths describing their combined effects. Fundamental to the Sepher Yetsirah is the knowledge and understanding of the Hegelian Dialectic, and of balance and harmony. In my experience, it is very rare for all three cards to appear in the same pile and be connected, so their presence can be taken to be an indication of unresolved issues in the life of the client. Magically, the positioning of these cards can be used to indicate ways of resolving Mem and Shin into Aleph. Mem and Shin together mean The Name.

The Double Letters

The Double Letters represent phonetics in the Hebrew language where each letter has a hard and soft pronunciation. We also see the dialectic at work here, as each letter has an opposite meaning depending on how it is pronounced. There are of course only seven letters, but Chapter Six of the Sepher Yetsirah discusses the Lunar Nodes, which is why we count nine, and not seven. The Lunar Nodes are not planets, but points in the plane of the ecliptic, and are used to predict eclipses. In Indian astrology, the Nodes are known as the Dragon's Head and Dragon's Tail, which is interesting because in the same chapter is mentioned the constellation Draco which encircles the Pole Star. In the same chapter, there are references to the Pole Star with the Earth suspended on a thread. This part of the Sepher Yetsirah may also be the inspiration for the projection of the Tarot onto the Heavens.

The Single Letters

The twelve single letters represent the twelve signs of the zodiac, and from this we can derive various body parts. These twelve letters also define the Cosmic Cube. Using the Opening of the Key spread, we can see how to use this particular system to define the personal Cosmic Cube for the reading – include the surrounding cards, cards 12 away, and cards that count onto each single letter. Since single letters can connect, we may see other patterns developing. This method has unlimited possibilities.

Minor Cards

The Minor Cards represent the corresponding sephiroth on the Tree of Life, excluding the Aces which as we have seen are separate from the Minor cards. One reason for separating the Aces is that by Temurah, Kether become Karet, "cut off". The four elements represent the four levels of the Tree of Life, so the magician can analyse the effect of an operation at a particular level of the Tree and of a particular Sephiroth.

The Princesses

There are two important strands of Kabbalist thought. One is the Sepher Yetsirah, while the other is the Bahir. Both figure in Crowley's workings. For example, his record of his visions of the thirty Enochian Aethyrs, The Vision and the Voice, is numbered Liber 418, and 418 is the numeration of the eighth Hebrew Letter Chet, and the Chariot Tarot card. The Chariot is the symbol of the ability to travel safely up through the spiritual realms, and is described in Ezekiel 1. A synonym for Chariot is Throne, and in the Opening of the Key spread, the Aces are the Thrones of the Princesses. The Princesses are associated with the "Palaces of Malkuth", a technical term for the seven cosmic realms. Both the Princesses and the Aces are said to rule the quadrants about the North Pole.

S.L. MacGregor Mathers, one of the founders of the Golden Dawn translated parts of the Zohar from Latin in his book, *The Kabbalah Unveiled*, which includes references to Palaces. Palace or HYKL in Hebrew has the same value as ADNY, 65. Traditionally when spoken out loud, YHVH is either replaced with a slight pause, or ADNY.

In The Book of Concealed Mystery, verse 32, McGregor makes absolutely clear the relationship between the Chariot, the Palaces and the four elements:

> *"The seven palaces answer to the 3ʳᵈ, 4ᵗʰ, 5ᵗʰ, 6ᵗʰ, 7ᵗʰ, 8ᵗʰ and 9ᵗʰ Sephiroth, operating through the respective orders of the angels into the spheres of the seven planets, Saturn, Jupiter, Mars, Sol, Venus, Mercury, and Luna. The four animals, or ChaiothHaQadesch, are the vivified powers of the four letters of the Tetragrammaton operating under the presidency of the first Sephira as the mainspring of primum mobile of creation. The four wheels are their correlatives under the second Sephira, on their four sides - namely, the four elements of the air, fire, water, and earth, which are the abodes of the spirits of the elements, the sylphs, salamanders, undines and gnomes, under the presidency of the tenth Sephira."*
> *S.L. MacGregor Mathers, The Kabbalah Unveiled*

The importance of this quotation is the explicit connections Mathers makes between several different systems (the sylphs, salamanders, etc are from a later system). A famous dictum within the Golden Dawn is that"Kether is in Malkuth after another way". Kether and Malkuth have an intimate connection. Mathers connects the palaces with YHVH, the Sephiroth, and the Chariot.

Card Counting

Now that I have given a general indication of how the different groups of cards in the Opening of the Key spread can be seen in the context of the Sepher Yetsirah, it is time to consider the reading techniques used, namely Card Counting and Pairing.

Both methods are described in the Sepher Yetsirah, and it would seem that Mathers or the anonymous author of the spread adapted the methods. Great care needs to be exercised at this point, as Kabbalism expressly forbids the use of "graven images", and many modern kabbalists frown upon the use of the hebrew alphabet on tarot cards. However, the world has moved on, and in the Opening of the Key spread, the cards are fanned out, so only a fairly small strip of each card is visible, except of course for the top card.

In this chapter I have been careful to define the groups of cards in a kabbalistic framework, but not by the usual terms. This is very important. Many times while analysing the Opening of the Key spread in a reading, I have had visions or thoughts that are not representative of the Divinatory Meanings of the cards. It was these experiences that made me continue with my efforts at understanding the mechanics of the spread.

Kabbalists believe that the manipulation of the letters of the Hebrew alphabet result in mystical experiences. It would seem that a parallel can be made to the Card Counting and Pairing performed in the Opening of the Key spread, but I have to add here that this can only be in the context of the reading – the usual questions tarot readers are asked are hardly likely to result in Visions of God!

Letter manipulation is described in the Sepher Yetsirah. The three keywords are Chakak, Chatzav and Tzaraf. Chakak involves writing; Chatzav denotes the formation of the letters, while Tzaraf indicates permutation. Writing and permuting the letters of the alphabet while in a meditative state can give rise to prophetic states.

Abraham Abulafia was one of the great Kabbalists who successfully used the techniques described in the Sepher Yetsirah, and the reader should read Aryeh Kaplan's books on the Sepher Yetsirah, and Meditation and Kabbalah for full details.

Now of course in a Tarot reading, we have two imperfect beings, the Reader and the Querent, so what benefit can be gained? As is well known, the teacher usually gains more than the students, so he will gain in knowledge of how the permutation of the cards can represent situations in the querent's life, while at the same be able to communicate better how the querent can improve the circumstances.

Card Counting

Quite how the GD came up with Card Counting is not clear, but there are Kabbalistic meditative techniques known as "jumping" and "skipping", discussed by Albotini who was familiar with Abulafia's methods. Skipping involves studying the gematria of a combination of letters, while when one uses other systems at the same time, one is "jumping".

CHAPTER ELEVEN

Fortune and Strength (Lust)

Fortune = 20, Kaph
Air, Jupiter, Double Letter

Strength or Lust = 9, Teth
Fire, Leo, Single Letter

29 means DKH is broken, and HDK, breakdown, overturn.

Eleven is Crowley's number of change and transformation, of Magick. Eleven is a powerful number as it is one beyond ten – it takes the magician out of the Tree of Life. Daath is said to be the eleventh sephirah which is the entrance to another Tree of Life or another Universe. In the rules of Gematria, an extra unit known as colel can be added to the value, which would give us 30, the number of Lamed, Adjustment, which is another important aspect to Crowley's system.

The Fortune card represents the universe in a state of continual change. The ten sephiroth are depicted on a wheel, in contrast to the Lust card. Much of this cards description in *The Book of Thoth* is taken up with a discussion of the Three

Gunas, which describe the transmutation of elements, an important concept in Elemental Dignities. The Wheel is associated with the Eye of Shiva 'whose opening annihilates the Universe' (Book of Thoth). The reader is referred to Crowley's Rite of Jupiter, which resembles the Fortune card.

With the Lust card (also known as Strength) the critical passage in *The Book of Thoth* is: *"Behind the figures of the Beast and his Bride are ten luminous rayed circles; they are the Sephiroth latent and not yet in order, for every new Aeon demands a new system of classification of the Universe."* This clearly relates to the concept of DKH (broken) and HDK (breakdown, overturn) and note that the same letters are used – K as the Fortune card, D for the Empress, and H for Aries, which can be seen as the Bride and Beast respectively. Since duality is such an important concept in the Book of Thoth, we have to see the concept of breakdown overturned into unification (marriage) and re-creation.

Daath

Daath, the 11th Sephira, whose existence depends on one's point of view, is mentioned obliquely in both Fortune and Lust. In the Fortune card, Crowley associates the Three Gunas with the Four Kerubs of the Sphinx, a reference to the Archangels of the Quarters and to Daath, while in the Lust card the Seraphim or serpents *"sent forth in every direction to destroy and re-create the world."* The Seraphim are also associated with the Caduceus.

While an Aeon can represent 2,000 years, it also works on the human scale, which would mark a change in consciousness. We might reasonably ask if the Book of Thoth represents the new system of classification, or a transitional state. Time will tell.

The Spirits of the Tarot

There are many sets of Spirits associated with the Tarot. The Kabbalistic angels and archangels have been covered in many books such as Dion Fortune's *Mystical Qabalah*, and are not included in this book. The relationship of the Enochian Spirits to the Tarot is also omitted here for reasons of space. This leaves the Goetia and the spirits of Crowley's Liber 231.

Goetia and the Holy Guardian Angel

Mention Goetic Spirits, and expect a frisson of fear or apprehension to run through the audience. At various times, during my own magical training, Goetic Spirits have appeared to me, but I have never performed any Goetic rituals, since to me the rituals represent a lot of hassle and effort, possibly taking months, with at best vague results, and at worst problems with 'possession'.

The nature of Goetic invocation will never result in the full agreement or assistance of the Spirit anyway. If the reader was brutally woken up at 3am, threatened with death and torture, or that one's relatives or loved ones would be tortured without compliance, and that the torturers could return at any time to demand more favours, would the reader fully and enthusiastically comply with what is required? I doubt it. Grudging compliance and thoughts of revenge at some point in the future is more likely.

An important aspect of the Opening of the Key Spread is that Spirits appear in groups rather than individually. I have not heard of any other method that is as powerful. Several days after Gaap and the other Goetic spirits appeared, I was chatting with a friend, an expert on Remote Viewing. I told him that the Goetic Spirits had appeared to me. He had never heard of them, so I explained that there were 72 of them, and the nature of Goetic invocation. We met up several days later, and he immediately wanted to discuss Goetia. He had remotely viewed them, and his first comment was that many of them looked like monsters! He said that they were immensely powerful – he wouldn't be tangling with them, except to ask very nicely... To me, it was apparent that a spirit was talking through him, since he was talking about the need for respect, avoiding threats of torture etc. As he was talking, we were both aware that we were surrounded by the 72 Spirits.

Several days after the Goetic Spirits first appeared to me, it became apparent that there was some friendly rivalry between them and the Spirits of Liber 231 – it was a case of 'anything you can do, I can do better'. The Goetic Spirits desire to be as available to the Tarot reader and magician as much as the Spirits of Liber 231, using the methods of the unaspected cards. The Goetic Spirits and Spirits of Liber 231 are only a tarot reading away.

Now before anyone accuses me of New Age claptrap, the Goetia solemnly tell me that they still have the awesome powers of destruction written about in Grimoires, and they will use them if required. If anyone feels terrified at this thought, 99.99% of all tarot readings I perform are just that, tarot readings.

Visible appearance of Goetic or Spirits of Liber 231 will only occur after a protracted period of study of all four sequences of cards, and since all 78 cards are included, there will always be checks and balances. Put another way, the balance of the four elements in the Tarot reading will represent the Spirits that can be evoked. There is always a microcosmic and macrocosmic aspect to magical work – the transformation for the client will always be reflected in a transformation in some way in the magician, and there will be some effect in the world at large.

For instance every time I see the Goetic spririt Gaap he appears hooded, just as in the Grimoire descriptions, my mind immediately turns to the Hermit card. Gaap confirms the connection, but it was not until I made progress in my understanding of Liber 231 and the formula of IAO that I could make the connection. I originally thought that Gaap was the secret ruler as signified by the Hermit, but it could be that the Goetia have a fundamental link to the Spirits of Liber 231, in that both are associated with meeting one's Holy Guardian Angel. Whatever the truth, and at these levels there will always be ambiguity, Crowley makes it clear that the Hermit is equated with the *"highest form of Mercury"*.

The Goetic spirits are well known to western magicians and students of tarot, but until now the methods of invoking the Goetia have been brutal and unsophisticated. The use of the Unaspected Minor cards in the Opening of the Key Spread changes this.

Liber 231

In January 2003, during a period of prolonged study and analysis of the sequences of cards used in this book, I had a strange dream. I was interrogated on the existence of a second Fool card by a group of spirits. I defended my case strongly – I had not heard of a second Fool card, and besides, the existence of two zeroes is impossible. After some days thought, I re-arranged the question, and considered the possibility that the Fool could have two functions. If everything is ejected from the Nothingness of the Fool, then could it be that the Fool was a Gate that also had the inverse function?

A day or two later, I was confronted with a spiritual problem that would not go away. I thought of the dream, and the possible solution, so I created a 'negative space'. Instantly, the problem disappeared, and simultaneously I received all 22 names of the Spirits, starting with Amprodius. A few days later, I heard about Donald Michael Kraig's new book *Tarot and Magick*. At the back of the book is an account of an invocation of Amprodius that nearly resulted in the death of the author. I had a book to write, but thoughts of *Liber 231* would not go away.

Very little has been written about *Liber 231*, except that there is a mystery surrounding the origin of the 44 sigils. This is a classic misdirection statement. Having worked on Liber 231 over the next months, it became clear that by focussing on the origin of the Sigils, the real import of *Liber 231* is completely missed. By analysing the 22 verses of *Liber 231* in the light of the Golden Dawn teachings and Crowley's own writings, a picture of the course and goal in attaining one's Holy Guardian Angel appears.

We do not know how Crowley discovered these fascinating spirits, but it seems to have happened during 1912, the year he wrote The Book of Lies. This book is an essay by Crowley on Gematria for the numbers zero to 93. After its publication the Head of the O.T.O. Theodor Reuss confronted Crowley for revealing the sex magic secrets of the Order, Crowley protested that he could not have revealed them because he had not reached the requisite level in the order, but Chapter 36 of the Book of Lies gives them away. In fact as the Supernal Triangle is replete with sexual imagery, so anyone who studies the Tree of Life long enough will eventually uncover them. My own contact with the Spirits of *Liber 231* suggests that their discovery did involve some kind of sex magic.

The first class of Spirit is ruled by Mercury, and the commentary on them forms the Book of Thoth. The names of most of the spirits can be deconstructed fairly easily, having Enochian words, and at least one Goetic spirit, but some of them may be anagrams of Greek words. Crowley seemed to be in anagram and punning mode with the names, having been recently working on the Book of Lies. The Coptic St added to some of the names is a Golden Dawn innovation, and indicates the influence of Kether.

In the first Knowledge Lecture of the Golden Dawn book, in which is discussed the 0=0 Neophyte Ritual in terms of Egyptian iconography, the following quotation from the Theban Recension appears:

> *"Concerning the exaltation of the Glorified Ones, of Coming and Going forth in the Divine Domain, of the Genies of the Beautiful land of Amentet. Of coming forth in the light of Day in any form desired, of Hearing the Forces of Nature by being enshrined as a living Bai."*
>
> *"The united with Osiris shall recite it when he has entered the Harbour. May glorious things be done thereby upon earth. May all the words of the Adept be fulfilled."*
>
> Israel Regardie, *The Golden Dawn*

"Asar in Ammenti" is part of the title of the 22 Mercurial Spirits. Asar is Osiris, God of the Dead, and in Golden Dawn parlance a symbol of balanced spiritual force harmonising the four elements. Amenti or Amentet is the Land of the Underworld and the name of the Goddess of the Underworld. In the Hall of Maat are the 42 Judges of the Dead who have to be named by the traveller on his journey. Since the Fool is numbered zero, we can postulate that the Judges are the two sets of 21 Major cards and the Fool, which would add up to 42. Thoth, Maat, the feather and the heart are all part of the description of the Hall of Maat, and appear in the verses of Liber 231.

On one level, we see that events in *Liber 231* parallels the Golden Dawn 0=0 Neophyte ceremony, which in turn is based upon the Hall of Maat, but Crowley incorporated many other levels of meaning within the text, which suits the aphoristic style. At a stroke he transformed the negative connotations (*"I have not committed murder…"*), which echoes the Ten Commandments (*"Thou shalt not…"*) into joyful progress towards enlightenment. There is another, perhaps more profound insight that can be gained here. Israel Regardie confirms that the 42 Judges each have an Overseer, the God Thoth and the Goddess Maat.

Regardie says that the Thoth and Maat are virtually indistinguishable, so we see that the Book of the Law and the Book of Thoth are two sides of the same coin. An enduring myth concerning the Tarot is that there is a Hall underneath the Sphinx, lined with images of the Tarot. While there is of course no evidence for this, we can use *Liber 231* as part of a powerful visualisation of a journey under the Sphinx to the Great Pyramid as part of an invocation to one's Holy Guardian Angel.

Crowleys Liber 671 is a description of the Neophyte 0=0 ceremony, and Liber 777 tells us that 671 is the number of the Gate, ADNY spelt in full, and Torah, the Law. 65 is the number of ADNY, My Lord, a title of the Holy Guardian Angel. Anglicisation and Metathesis of ThROA and ThORA, the Gate and the Law, gives us Taro Rota Tora Ator, so now we have the implicit linkage:

Hall of Maat = Neophyte Ceremony = Holy Guardian Angel = Taro = Gate = Law.

Though the Opening of the Key Spread is particularly suited for divination of mundane events, it was used by Golden Dawn Adepts as a means of contacting their Holy Guardian Angel. The methods for contacting the HGA were never made explicit, but it seems that meditation on the Pairing and Counting methods discussed in this book are part it. Although there do not appear to be any magical analogues to these techniques, they can be found in kabbalistic methods of textual analysis. So Pairing the verses of *Liber 231* from the outer to the inner was conducted, and then the similarity to *"The Suggestive Correspondences From the Hebrew Alphabet"* page 40 of *Liber 777* was noted. These correspondences show the initiatory meanings of the letters.

Amentet is the region of the Dead, while the Asar (Osiris) and Amentet, God and Goddess respectively rule over Amentet. The enlightened individual can be seen as 'dead' to the rest of the population, so Liber 231 represents a journey through Amentet resulting in the Knowledge with one's Holy Guardian Angel. The method of attaining the HGA is through sex magic, as seen from column XIX in *Liber 777*, where the combination of Asar and Asi is found in Yesod, and Crowley notes that they represent the phallus and vulva respectively; but also Seti (Set) is included as the Spine, which is a clear reference to Kundalini. Crowley was well acquainted with the Eastern tradition of making the first verse an overview of the entire book or chapter. IAO can be seen not only as the formula of attaining the Holy Guardian Angel, but as representing Kundalini rising between the columns of Ida and Pingala, the Pillars of Solomon in the Temple, and depicted in the Priestess tarot card. The quotation from the Theban Recension mentioned above, says *"...Hearing the Forces of Nature..."* which goes some way to explaining the 'thunders' mentioned in verse 1 of *Liber 231*.

Throughout the history of spiritual and magical endeavours, the importance of spiritual development over acquisition of magical powers is constantly emphasized. To aspire for magical powers without the concomitant spiritual development is akin to black magic. While the Tarot unifies the magical powers of Enochian, Goetia and *Liber 231*, until now, the methods of contacting one's own Holy Guardian Angel have remained oblique. The paradox of achievement in attaining the Holy Guardian Angel is contact with myriad other spirits. To do this any other way is to put the cart before horse. These methods unify the saying *"Rota Taro Orat Tora Ator"*, *"the wheel of the tarot speaks the law of Hathor"*.

When the the first four letters in the word Tarot are placed on the four spokes of a wheel, they can be read in four different ways: Taro, Rota, Orat, Tora. The meanings of these words are somewhat obscure, but they might have been understood by Crowley to signify, respectively, the Way, the Wheel, the Word and the Law.

The word for 'law' is the Torah, so those who are not happy with the Thelemic system can use the Kabbalistic version. It may be of interest to note that 'Tora' appears on many versions of the High Priestess, and it was the Spirit Gargophias who first appeared to the author during the writing of this book.

Taro, Rota, Orat and Tora are related to the four Living Creatures of Ezekiel, which rule over the four directions and four elements, the Chariot, Fortune and Universe cards all have them depicted on them.

ADNY – the starting symbol of Liber 231

The creation of the 44 symbols in Liber 231 is considered to be a mystery, yet *Book IV, Magic* gives clues. ADNY or Adonai, meaning 'my Lord' is a term referring to the Holy Guardian Angel (HGA), and it appears in the last verse of *Liber 231*. Using the traditional mantra of the Golden Dawn, *"Malkuth is in Kether after another way";* we know that the last and first Sephiroth are intimately connected. In *Book IV Part 2*, ADNY is discussed in *Chapter 8, "The Sword"*, which is on the face of it rather surprising. Detailed analysis of the Sword is beyond the scope of this book, but several phrases stand out. The sword is used to control demons such as Goetia, and it is the engine of division. Crowley says the sword is generally pointed downwards, because if it is raised towards the Crown (Kether), it is not a sword, because Kether cannot be divided. If however, the sword is held erect with both hands, it becomes the flame of Shin, the 21st letter, but there is a warning:

"The Magician cannot wield the Sword unless the Crown is on his head"
Aleister Crowley, Book IV Part 2

In other words, the Magician should have crossed the Abyss and he has the authority of Kether. The use of the Sword as division is interesting because there are two sets of Spirits in *Liber 231*. The alchemical phrase *"solve et coagula"* which appears in the Thoth Tarot is vital, since Crowley points out that

> *"Solvé is destruction, but so is Coagula. The aim of the Magus is to destroy his partial thought by uniting it with the Universal Thought, not to make a further breach and division in the Whole."*
> Aleister Crowley, Book of Thoth

On the blade of the Sword should be etched the Notariqon AGLA, *"Ateh Gibor Leolahm Adonai, To thee be the Power unto the Ages, O my Lord."*

The acid used to eat into the steel is vitriol, *"Visita Interiora Terrae Rectificando Invenies occultum lapidem"*, which appears on the Thoth Art card.

The Sword of Adonai *"hath four blades, the blade of the thunderbolt, the blade of the Pylon, the blade of the Serpent, the blade of the Phallus" (Liber LXV)*. The symbols for Aleph and Tzaddi in the Spirits of Mercury in *Liber 231* have a four-sided blade, or Swastika. Aleph is of course the first letter, while Tzaddi is related to the Thoth Star card (which has not been updated to reflect the injunction in Liber AL). The Swastika is based upon Geburah since the structure is the magic square of Mars, related to destruction. An obscure comment on the five tatvas in the 5 Disks is illuminated *"... these hold together, on a very low plane, an organism which would otherwise disrupt completely."*

The symbol for Aleph has a circle at the centre, which is the symbol of Malkuth, the four elements united, while the four dots can be seen as Bindus or points from which creation originates. The markings at the end of the lines can be seen as symbols of the Sword of Adonai. The symbol for Tzaddi is more complex, but in the top left corner is the flaming Sword working down through the Sephiroth. The Sword as symbol of Air is related to the Son, or BN, the secret name of Assiah, while 'O' is of course AYN, symbol of Nothing, beyond the Veil. Crowley of course knew his Bible well, and 52, the number of BN has interesting correspondences in Hebrew: Father and Mother; Supernal Mother; Holy Guardian Angel of Job. There is a connection to the whirling of the Sword at the Gate of Eden since OBN is 122, the number of GLGLYM, whirlings. Surrounding the swastika are four spirals (*"Creation is a spiral force"*, Book of Thoth). These four spirals are developed in the two symbols for Tau, The Universe, on which Crowley says:

"The first and most obvious characteristic of this card is that it comes at the end of all, and is therefore the complement of the Fool."
Aleister Crowley, Book of Thoth

As previously discussed, these two symbols of Tau represent IAO and ADNY.

The analysis of ADNY in *Book IV* makes clear the relationship between Aleph and Tzaddi, and at it this point it is useful to note that between the two sets of symbols, there is a comparison table starting with – *"Compare Aleph with Tzaddi..."* The natural inclination is to compare the Mercury Spirit with the Serpent spirit, but the analysis above suggests that the comparison is **within** the tables.

The Sword as Division is also the Sword of Union, so in some way, perhaps beyond the Abyss in the Supernal Triangle, these two sets of Spirits are conjoined.

Viewing the sigils of the Spirits, assuming that the comparison is within the tables, we can make several tentative interpretations. The comparisons may be Crowley looking at the Spirits of Mercury and noting the resemblance. Certainly the method does not work so well for the Spirits of the Serpent. Alternatively, the second symbol may have been created by the first. Another interpretation is that the comparison table is actually a sequential record of the creation of the Mercury symbols. To clarify the Table, here is the transliteration;

Compare	A and Tz
	B and G
	G and B
	D and O
	H and Ch
	V and K
	Z and D
	Ch andH
	T and Sh
	Y and M
	K and V
	L and S
	M and S
	N and Sh
	S and Z
	O and P
	P and Q
	Tz and A

Compare   Q and P
               R and Z
               Sh and T
               Th and B

You will notice that six pairs of letters are mentioned twice (once in each combination) an examination of these proves illuminating:

The gematria of Aleph/Tzaddi is 91, the sum of the numbers 1 to 13, the Mystic Number of Kether as Achad, and the number of Paths in the Supernal Beard; a tree, Amen, the Ephod and YHVH ADNY. As well as the Archangel of Geburah, we also have the Daughter Kore, relating to Malkuth. There are 91 chapters in the Book of Lies, and depending on how one counts them, the number of Enochian Governors.

BG means 'back', which could suggest the reverse side of the Tree of Life, or to return. Five is the number of Geburah, already discussed.

HCh is 13, the number of Paths in the Supernal Beard mentioned above, it is also Love and Unity, Emptiness, and significantly 'Thunder', mentioned in the Verses of *Liber 231*.

VK is 26, the number of YHVH and the number of the Sephiroth of the Middle Pillar, which represents a Sword. Another word is Vision, while KBD is the husband of Lillith.

ShT is 309, which can be translated as Fire Snake or Set, the name of Pan, Satan or Saturn (see the Fool card in the Book of Thoth). 309 is also the number of a field.

PQ is 180, number of a spring or fountain, and significantly, 'front', as opposed to BG 'back'.

The interpretation of AGLA has interesting connotations particularly in the New Aeon predicted in the Book of The Law, since it has '... *power unto the Ages...*' or Aeons. That power of division is represented in the two sets of Spirits in Liber 231. The gematria of AGLA, 35, is 'boundary, limit' and 'he will go'. In other words, the power of the Aeon is to go beyond the limit or boundary of Time, which is of course eternity.

Liber 231, IAO and the Holy Guardian Angel

Understanding the Sigils and Names of the 44 Spirits in *Liber 231* has always posed problems. There are several websites that give descriptions of the Sigils, but none undergo a serious analysis of the meaning of them. In Nightside of Eden, Kenneth Grant was the first to publish details of the spirits, and this inspired Linda Falorio to create a set of 22 Major cards based on them. However, the text of Liber 231 gives two Formulae of magick that are closely related to the Holy Guardian Angel. In the first verse, IAO appears, while in the last verse we have ADNI. Furthermore, the name of the Serpent Spirit contains iao at its heart. For some time, I considered that these were enough clues, but Crowley sought to hammer the message home in the sigils too. Look at the sigils for the Universe card - Thantifaxath and Thath'th'thithOthuth-thiST (The latter can be read in part as 'thath thith thoth' which contains an anagram of IAO, in other words the Holy Guardian Angel terminated by Tau, the last letter of the alphabet).

Most commentators describe both sigils as batteries connected by wires, which, for want of anything better I was happy to go along with. While meditating on the significance of IAO and ADNI in *Liber 231*, I cast my eyes over the sigils, and in a flash I saw what they represented. Quite simply, they are abstract representations of IAO and ADNI respectively. 'I' and 'O' are uppercase, joined by a lowercase 'a'. ADNI is not quite so easy, but the centre symbol looks like a 'D', the perpendicular tortoise is an 'a'; the 'n' is more abstract, ending with one of the 'i's, and then the final 'I'. It may of course be that there is a doubling of the letters in ADNI, since there is sufficient ambiguity in the depiction. Study of IAO and ADNI in *Book IV, Magick*, shows that there is an extra magical formulae, FIAOF, which illuminates the Serpent name for V, Vuaretza – [a secret name follows]. Since there had to be the textual clues, I believe the secret name in Vuaretza is FIAOF.

Before we enter into a deeper analysis of these magical formulae, it is worth looking at the gematria and related documents. IAO is 81: ALYM 'Gods', ANKY 'I', AP, 'anger, wrath, nose'. KSA 'throne', PA 'here, hither'. ADNI 'My Lord' is 65, 'The number of Abra-Melin Servitors of Magot and Kore' , AVChYM weasels, HYKL Palace, HLL shone, gloried, praised (Halleluyah), HS to keep silence, MKH a beating, striking. The following number, 66 is the number of the Qlippoth and of the 'Great Work', and is the summation of 1 to 11. Adding up 81 and 65 we get 146, which is SVP limit, end, boundless, and appears in AYN SVP AVR. BBA QMA First Gate is also significant, as is OVLM, World.

We can now see that the spirits of the Serpent or Mercury appear as Gods within the Self, sitting on Thrones, which is in itself an indication of Binah, while the Qliphotic Spirits can appear demonic or as animals. I am not entirely happy with use of Qliphotic, since the spirits appear to me as joyful. The combination of the two names signifies part of the Negative Veil, AYN SVP AVR, and I direct the reader to Crowley's discussion of the Naples Arrangement in the Book of Thoth. The gematria values of 231 are no less interesting. In *Liber 777*, 231 start with "Right handed Svastika, drawn on Square of Mars" which is precisely the sigil for Aleph! The Square of Mars is a magic square 5x5, and symbolises Geburah.

One of the prime objectives for the Golden Dawn Adept when performing the Opening of the Key Spread was contact with his Higher Genius, known as the Holy Guardian Angel. Just how this was supposed to be achieved is not clear in the Golden Dawn literature, but since it has been discovered that the fully Unaspected Major cards using the counting technique represent influence from higher levels, and that the Spirits of *Liber 231* are keen to make contact with the Diviner, we are closer to an answer. In the first verse of *Liber 231* is IAO, the formula for contacting one's Holy Guardian Angel.

Other commentators of the Tarot that mention *Liber 231* say that the origins of this document is shrouded in mystery, but in *Magick*, Aleister Crowley is open about the nature of IAO. The Formula has the Fool between the Hermit and the Devil. The Hermit is known as a secret master, and it represents the hidden penis, while the Devil is Pan, and the erect penis. That the method of gaining knowledge of one's HGA is sexual has been written about. If one had doubts, 81, the value of IAO is the square of 9, Yesod, which represents the sexual organs. The Trinity cannot abide on its own, so Crowley created the Formula of FIAOF, where F (or V) as the Son is the Hierophant, representing the New Age. Germane to IAO is Liber Stellae Rubeae, and its rubric is worth quoting in this context:

> *"A Secret Ritual of Apep, the Heart of IAO-OAI, Delivered unto V.V.V.V.V. for His Use in a Certain Matter of Liber Legis, and Written Down under the Figure LXVI"*
> *Aleister Crowley, Liber 66*

IAO-OAI is the formula that represents the two sets of 22 Spirits that comprise Liber 231. IAO indicates Magical processes, while OAI represents mystical processes. There is evidence in the title of Liber 231, where we have the Spirits of Mercury The Trinity cannot abide on its own, so Crowley created the Formula of FIAOF, where F (or V) as the Son is the Hierophant, representing the New Age.

There is evidence in the title of *Liber 231*, where we have the Spirits of Mercury (Mercury rules Virgo, the Hermit), while Carcerum is a form of Carcer, the Geomantic symbol equated with Capricorn, the Devil). Liber 231 displays a certain amount of ambiguity concerning sexuality – for example, the reader is not certain if Asar or Asi is male or female. A footnote in Crowley's vision of the Second Aethyr ARN, makes it clear that Pan, who is associated with both the Fool and the Devil cards, has a feminine or androgyne equivalent, known as Babalon.

The verses of *Liber 231* appear to be the synthesis of the formula IAO-OAI. Certainly the starting line of *Liber 66* gives a hint:

> *"Apep deifieth Asar".*
> *Aleister Crowley, Liber 66*

Apep is the Serpent, while Asar is Osiris, and we have already established that Osiris represents the balanced forces of all four elements present. The Serpent can be seen in several modes; that of the Serpent winding through all 22 Paths of the Tree of Life from Malkuth to Kether, while the Serpent is the Kundalini energy in the spine, or it can be associated with the Constellation Draco around the Pole Star. (The lightning mentioned in *Liber 231* is the Lightning Flash or Flaming Sword where the Sephiroth are connected from Kether to Malkuth). *Liber 66* is considered to be a manual on sex magic, which need not be discussed here, but I would like to draw the reader's attention to several passages that have relevance to *Liber 231*:

> *"I who reveal the ritual am IAO and OAI; the Right and the Averse. These are alike unto me"*
> *Aleister Crowley, Liber 66*

The Right and the Averse are titles that could be applied to the two sets of spirits in Liber 231, while the next line is critical since Crowley seems to be saying they are no different to him, or it may mean that he identifies with both. A few lines later, the identity of the A in IAO is revealed:

> *"I, Apep the Serpent, am the heart of IAO. Isis shall await Asar, and I in the midst."*
> *Aleister Crowley, Liber 66*

This line is different to the first line, where Apep is the heart of IAO-OAI.

If the reader is in any doubt as to the importance of IAO to the Spirits of Liber 231, look at the name of the first Geni of *Liber 231*, Aou-iao-uoa.

Malai, the name of the 13th Spirit, appears twice in the 'infernal adorations', and it is translated in ARN as 'staggered' The list of 'nonsense' words comes from Crowley's vision of the 2nd Aethyr, ARN, while the ai suffix that appears in other names is common to the litany. It could be that AI, which is of course part of AIO, is useful purely because the gematria is 11, the number of Magick. An alternative interpretation of Malai would be 'the Magick of Lam', the spirit who appeared to Crowley. From this we can infer another meaning to IAO – the Magick of Pan or Babalon.

We are now in a position to understand the first line of *Liber 231*:

> *"Apep, the Serpent, the heart of IAO, dwelleth in ecstasy in the secret place of the thunders. Between Osiris and Isis he abideth in joy."*
> Aleiester Crowley, *Liber 231*

The two phrases 'dwelleth in ecstasy' and 'abideth in joy' signify that the two sets of 22 spirits are joyful.

How do we reconcile the joyful nature of the spirits of Liber 231 with the Gothic descriptions of the spirits in Kenneth Grant's *Nightside of Eden?* As an Adept and Head of his own occult organisation, Kenneth Grant may feel constrained in his discussions. Linda Falorio, creator of the Shadow Tarot inspired by Kenneth Grant's description of the Spirits of Liber 231, continued the lurid descriptions of the spirits, but when she discusses the divinatory meanings of the tarot, she articulates many of the ideas that come to me in the course of a reading. The starkest difference may come down to the method of invocation. Kenneth Grant uses traditional methods that may be Goetic in origin, where the Magician determines in advance the Spirit to be invoked, and commands it to visible appearance using the usual threats and coercion, while in this book, the spirits spontaneously appear as a result of analysis of the unaspected cards in the context of the entire reading.

The Golden Dawn Neophyte Ceremony

The intertwining of Tarot with *Liber 231* and the 0=0 Neophyte Ceremony has interesting implications for the Tarot reader and Magician since the setting of the Neophyte Ceremony is the basis for all magical operations within the Golden Dawn. The General Exordium is the structural basis for the ritual, which is reflected in the paired verses of *Liber 231*. The extent to which Aleister Crowley was aware, consciously or unconsciously of the basis of *Liber 231* is unclear, but prolonged meditation on *Liber 231* provided inspiration for a unique Tarot spread that can be used for divination, the divinatory basis for determining a magical operation or ceremonial ritual, and the means for determining and rectifying mistakes made during these rituals (see appendix).

The layout and furnishings of the Neophyte Ceremony is based upon Egyptian Temples, and Admission to the Candidate in the Judgment Hall of Osiris, where the Candidate has to pass the 42 Assessors. According to Pat Zalewski, clairvoyant vision holds that the 42 Assessors appear back to back in two columns. The Assessors have animal heads and hold a sword. They rotate slowly, and their function is to create vortices in the ceremony. The vortices enable judgment of the candidate. There seems to be a Golden Dawn tradition that the Assessors follow and watch the candidate, and if he or she is found wanting, they sever the link to the Order with the sword. The Assessors can also bar the candidate from Outer to the Inner Order.

The Double Cube

While *Liber 231* can be seen as the Goddess representing the Temple, there are other parallels within the 0=0 Ceremony. The mystic circumambulation occurs around the doubled cube Altar, so we see that the Tarot reading represents the spiral energy around the Altar. The starting point will be on one face of the dark cube, and the end will be on same side of the white cube. The clockwise progress from dark to light represents spiritual evolution, while the reverse process from light to dark represents the descent of matter. In some respects, there are parallels to kundalini energy, so if the modules were split into two, starting on opposite sides of the cube, we have a powerful system of spiritual change.

Mystic Circumambulation

The Mystic Circumambulation around the Altar comprises three and a half turns, while the spread above only manages two circuits when starting from the centre of the Altar, or two and a half circuits when starting from one side. Where is the extra circuit? The answer lies in the Equinox and Solstice Ceremonies of the Golden Dawn, which tie in the convoluted forces around the North Pole with the progress of the Sun through the year. The ceremonies are based upon the 0=0 arrangement, and draw down the power of the Sun through the natural framework of nature of the power and unity of order for spiritual and material benefit. The Spring Equinox is a period of outreach for the group where Isis gives birth. The Autumn Equinox is ruled by Venus, and is a time for the individual search for the Higher Self, and in the Egyptian Mysteries represents the death and resurrection of Osiris.

One objective of the ceremonies is to balance the four elemental energies before projection into the new season, which is aided by the circumambulation, but the primary objective is to establish a magical link to the Hidden or Secret Chiefs.

In the second part of the Consecration Ceremony of the Vault of the Adepti, the scene changes from an Egyptian theme to that of tomb of Christian Rozenkreutz, mythical leader of the Rosicrucian movement. Remarkably, Book T, the title of the Tarot in the Golden Dawn is part of the ceremony where the transition is made from the Egyptian to the Rosicrucian. At this juncture, the Chief Adept has been placed on the Cross to suffer the sins of the previous season. There is also a critical change in rulership from the 'Great Avenging Angel HRU' to 'HUA, the Great Angel' **after** the presentation of Book "T":

Chief Adept: (while still bound) "I invoke Thee, the Great Avenging Angel HRU to confirm and strengthen all Members of this Order during the ensuing Revolution of the Sun, to keep them steadfast in the Path of rectitude and self-sacrifice, and to confer upon them the power of discernment, that they may choose between the evil and the good, and try all things of doubtful or fictitious seeming with sure knowledge and sound judgment."

Second Adept: "Let the Chief descend from the Cross of Suffering."
He is released and the Cross removed.
Second Adept: "Merciful Exempt Adept, I, on behalf of the Second Order, request you to re-invest yourself with the insignia of your high office, which alone has entitled you to offer yourself unto the High Powers as surety for the Order."

Chief Adept reclothes. Three adepts enter Vault, roll Altar aside, open lid of Pastos, put Book "T" upon table. Chief steps into the Pastos, and stands facing the door. The Three Adepts join Wands and Cruces.
Chief Adept: "I invoke Thee, HUA, the Great Angel who art set over the operations of this secret Wisdom, to strengthen and establish this Order in its search for the Mysteries of the Divine Light. Increase the Spiritual perception of the Members and enable them to rise beyond that lower Self-hood which is nothing, unto that Highest Self-hood which is God the Vast One."
Isreal Regardie, The Golden Dawn

One significant factor in the presence of the Tarot is that it is the full deck, in book form, whereas in other rituals, pathworking means that only a certain number of the Major cards are present.

The third and final circuit of the Tarot Spread is invisible, but the extra four positions can be visualised by the Tarot reader. The entire process is described by Crowley's mentor Alan Bennett:

Thus can our Science teach us wherefore the Door of Venus, Daleth, is the gateway of Initiation: that one planet whose symbol alone embraceth the 10 Sephiroth; the Entrance to the Shrine of our Father C.R.C., the Tomb of Osiris; the God Revealer, coming, moreover, by the Central Path of Samekh through the midst of the Triangle of Light. And the lock which guards that Door is as the Four gates of the Universe.

And the Key is the Ankh, Immortal Life – the Rose and Cross of Life; and the symbol of Venus.
Allan Bennett, Notes on Genesis

The Opening of the Key Spread is now revealed as the Tarot Key, the Key to communing with the Holy Guardian Angel, the Key to the Secret Chiefs. Look on the back cover of the Book of Thoth. There we see the God Thoth holding the Sceptre of the Major Adept, the Phoenix symbol of rebirth and resurrection in his right hand. On the outstretched left hand is a lotus flower upon which is an Ankh, surrounded by the TARO, symbol of the Holy Guardian Angel.

Meditations

The Meditations presented here have been developed from the pairing of the Major cards, the pairing of the verses of Liber 231, and the pairing of the initiatory correspondences of the Hebrew alphabet. The number of pairings total 11, the number of Change and of Magick. Each pairing is also associated with a stage of the Neophyte Ritual, the basis of Golden Dawn magic.

Thus we see that *Liber 231* was created on the basis of the study of the Kabbalah, the use of the rituals of the Golden Dawn to attain the Holy Guardian Angel, and the names of Enochian Spirits. The reader is refered to the description of the magical weapons in the commentary on Column XLI in *Liber 777*. Rather than try to analyse the sigils, I suggest the reader study the magical weapons and discover the abstract forms of these weapons that can be found in the Sigils of Liber 231.

Part 1. General Exordium
The Speech in the Silence:

The Assessors
Amprodius: A, the heart of IAO, dwelleth in ecstasy in the secret place of the thunders. Between Asar and Asi he abideth in joy.

Thantifaxath : And in the heart of the Sphinx danced the Lord Adonai, in

His garlands of roses and pearls making glad the concourse of things; yea, making glad the concourse of things.

The Vision

In the black flashes the black emptiness of Amprodius from whose absence projects the arcing of the entire Universe of Thantifaxath. Sitting in the Akashic Egg of blackness, we feel points of starlight from ancient civilizations energising our aura. Kundalini flows through the spine in three pillars. The energy shoots through our head, transforming into the winged caduceus, spiralling in loops through eternity. From heights beyond the Pole Star, transformed energy returns vortexing around the awakening celestial Dragon. Draco ripples and fluctuates into four forms – He creeps, He loops, He flies, He revolves. The energies spiral round the earth, dipping into the Apex of the Great Pyramid to be revived by Thantifaxath. Deep within the Earth, points of light crackle and roar, shining brilliantly, coalescing into new crystal structures that function as batteries energised from the Earth's energy, Thantifaxath's gift to mankind. Crystals energise the aura, giving great power to the magician, his path clear between Heaven and Earth working his magick. Harmonising our energy with the sigil of Thantifaxath, He provides the Earthing current to the silent scream of Amprodius. The circuit of energy running and returning flows, purifying our Being.

The Challenge

Now is the time to initiate the Great Work, receiving Divine Inspiration and to respond to Spirit. Great patience and perseverance is required. This is the time to purify and prepare your Body and the Temple.

Part 2. General Exordium

The Words against the Son of Night.

In his Confessions, Crowley says:

> *Note Christ as the Healer, and also his own expression, "The son of Man cometh as a thief in the night"; and also this scripture (Matt. XXIV, 27), "For as the lightning cometh out of the east and shineth even unto the west, so shall also the coming of the Son of Man be."* One of the characteristics of Mercury is theft.

The Assessors

Baratchiel: "The lightnings increased and the Lord Tahuti stood forth. The Voice came from the Silence. Then the One ran and returned."

Shalicu: "Then also the pyramid was builded so that the Initiation might be complete."

The Vision

The circulated energy arises from the Adept through Draco, beyond the Pole Star back to the Great Pyramid at Giza, where the energy transforms the Earth. Vortices echo and return to the deep past, resurrecting the Old Ones. The Voice of Amprodius is now audible (heard by whom?), projecting chaotic energy that is captured and juggled by Baratchiel. As the chaos becomes ordered, the circulating energy heats up the Great Pyramid, which glows incandescent. Shalicu dances an ancient dance of infinity perpendicular to the infinite loop of energy, thrilling to the power of Amprodius as it radiates darkness. The New Aeon is an Old Aeon, far too old for even the most persistent race memory to comprehend. The initial experience of the creation of the four elements is of destruction as they prepare the way for the New Aeon. The balanced ordering of the elements swirling around the Adept transforms every fibre of his being, every muscle, every sinew as the Holy Fire rushes up through him. Reborn through Death, he no longer has need of magical weapons – he is an instrument of the four elements. He has mastered Time.

The Challenge

Time to trust the Voice of Spirit. Spirit teaches, heals and nourishes indirectly in preparation for the challenges of facing and ruling one's enemies. Your voice is your weapon. The true warrior remains hidden. To win friends is better than fighting. Maintain inner balance so all decisions is decisive. Master Fire. Learn lessons from the past to prepare for the future.

Part 3. General Exordium

The Voice of Thoth before the Universe in the presence of the Eternal Gods:

The Assessors

Gargophias: Now hath Nuit veiled herself, that she may open the gate of her sister.

Rafliflu: Then the sun did appear unclouded, and the mouth of Asi was on the mouth of Asar.

The Vision

In the thick darkness, you stand at the Gates of a vast Temple before the Great Sphinx. A Gatekeeper appears. He motions you forward, but the Gate slams shut. You wait, contemplating your Fate, meditating on your past actions and intentions for the future. You are lost in time, but eventually you become aware that darkness no longer surrounds you. The Sun rises showing that the Gate has swung open, inviting you to enter.

The Challenge

Although on the early stages of the Work, you are required to inspire others, bring them to the Light, and to help your fellow travellers. New windows of opportunity open up that must be explored. Strange dreams. Live with change. If you have not learned the lessons of Baratchiel and Shalicu, lawsuits await, or your freedoms will be curtailed. Use new visions to plan for the future. Will promises of wealth distract you from your path?

Part 4. General Exordium

The Formulas of Knowledge:

The Assessors

Dagdagiel: The Virgin of God is enthroned upon an oyster-shell: she is like a pearl, and seeketh 70 to her 4. In her heart is Hadith the invisible glory.

Qulielfi: By her spells she invoked the Scarab, the Lord Keph-Ra, so that the waters were cloven and the illusion of the towers was destroyed.

The Vision

Just inside the Gate your progress is barred by Anubis who asks for the passwords. By your side has appeared a Guide. Ahead, two Towers appear swathed in swirling, coruscating darkness, radiating fear. Your Guide gives the password, you enter the Hall. Far ahead a dim light appears radiating peace. As your Guide ushers you forward, you become aware of vast Presences about you, and before you a narrow white line glows enticing you forward.

The Challenge

You are the Guide; bless and maintain new magical links. Explore your gift of healing – people will come with their problems, do you have answers? Your voice must express truth in its evocation of new beginnings. Practice divination, practice counselling, and search for lost knowledge. Explore the dark night of the Soul. Realise that Truth brings Illusion. Can you command Spirits to speak the truth?

Part 5. General Exordium

The Wisdom of Breath:

The Assessors

Hemeterith: Now riseth Ra-Hoor-Khuit, and dominion is established in the Star of Flame.

Tzuflifu: Transformed, the holy virgin appeared as a fluidic fire, making her beauty into a thunderbolt.

The Vision

As you move forward a gust of wind takes your breath away. Before, is the appearance of a Holy Child bathed in flames, held by his Mother. Thunder and Lightning play about them. You look to the face of the Child, and it is your own.

The Challenge

Turn your eyes to the night sky. Learn the knowledge of the stars. See the fine line between illumination and despair. How painful will be the birthpangs? Will this Child be a monster or Avatar? From where will the unexpected renewal come from? What new parent child relationship will evolve – will you learn from the past or merely repeat mistakes? After the birth there will be many, many battles to overcome – will you emerge Victorious?

Part 6. General Exordium

The Radix of Vibration

The Assessors

Uriens: Also is the Star of Flame exalted, bringing benedictions to the Universe.

Parfaxitas: He smote the towers of wailing; he brake them in pieces in the fire of his anger, so that he alone did escape from the ruin thereof.

The Vision

The Child smiles, his hand reaches out to you. You come closer; a crack of thunder heralds an explosion in the Crown of your head. Your body disintegrates, flesh falls away, to become a body of Light.

The Challenge

Bridge the vast gulf between you and your Self. Discipline yourself to receive the Knowledge from High. This is a marathon not a sprint. To create you have to destroy, to transform, to attract, to channel raw sexual energy to exalted levels. Abandon faulty plans, thwart the plans of your enemies, and use their energy for your own designs.

Part 7. General Exordium

The Shaking of the Invisible

The Assessors

Zamradiel: Here then beneath the winged Eros is youth, delighting in the one and the other. He is Asar between Asi and Nepthi.

A'Ano'nin: The Lord Khem arose. He who is holy among the highest, and set up his crowned staff for to redeem the universe.

The Vision

Your body still quivering, you look to your hands created anew then you realise you have a new body. Above, angels dance in joy; you look toward the earth, you are now atop a high mountain, bathed in irradiated light. You find yourself back in the Hall, and in the Light the Egyptian Gods come alive.

The Challenge

Your enemies routed, you increase your territory and power. Reach out, be One with your world, but make sure the links you have are the one's you desire. Life is a game, Maya; superficiality and serious are easy bedfellows. Which is which? Be decisive. With a common creation, everything can be anything else. Is your Will strong enough? For what use is your Will for? Power? Influence? Fame? Will you reform? Will you repress?

Part 8. General Exordium

The Rolling Asunder of the Darkness

The Assessors

Characith: He rideth upon the chariot of eternity: the white and the black are harnessed to his car. Therefore he reflecteth the Fool and the sevenfold veil is revealed.

Saksalim: And a mighty angel appeared as a woman, pouring vials of woe upon the flames, lighting the pure stream with her brand of cursing. And the iniquity was very great.

The Vision

At the entrance of a vast Chamber Anubis guides you to the Goddess Thmaest, ruler of the Hall of Truth, Horus by her side. A chariot appears pulled by horses, and you climb aboard. Before the chariot can move Thmaest bars your path, her countenance terrible to behold. She curses and wails at your sins while the chariot moves toward her. Just as you are unable to endure her imprecations anymore, her countenance becomes benign. Your energies balanced, you pass the two columns of Assessors, each revolving on their thrones.

The Challenge

You rule your territory, but have you the power to explore? What hidden dangers remain? Do your fears still control you? What other territories need your attention? The Journey has barely begun, and you may fail to reach your Holy Grail. Although you travel alone, you will have to inspire and lead your colleagues. How will you separate reality and illusion for them? If you cannot destroy forces against your group, can you nullify to allow safe passage when all is against you? The difficult and dangerous path is better than the simple route followed by others. Will you remember the Way?

Part 9. General Exordium

The Becoming Visible of Matter

The Assessors

Lafcursiax: Also the lady Maat with her feather and sword abode to judge the righteous. For Fate was already established.

Niantiel: Also Asar was hidden in Amenti: and the Lords of Time swept him with the sickle of death.

The Vision

The Procession becomes an ecstatic experience of joy. The vision of the Gods strengthens – they are real to you. You see your births and deaths in the vastness of Time. You see friends and family as travellers on a similar journey. You meet those of whom who have passed on before.

The Challenge

The trials and adversities of the Sojourn increases fellowship, and their respect for you gains. Balance the needs of your self with the needs of the group, and the goals still to reach. Wise counsel and balanced thinking is never easy. During the long journey there will be time for mysticism, contemplation, and philosophy. Raise your mind beyond the mundane. See the never-ending cycles of sex, life and death. Embrace change.

Part 10. General Exordium

The Piercing of the Coils of the Stooping Dragon:

The Assessors

Yamatu: Also the Priest veiled himself, lest his glory be profaned, lest his word be lost in the multitude.

Malkunofat: Then the holy one appeared in the greater water of the North: as a golden dawn did he appear, bringing benediction to the fallen universe.

The Vision

After another Death you find yourself outside the Sphinx, and before Great Pyramid of Gizeh. Above the Pyramid is the Pole Star surrounded by the swirling of the Dragon as if in a Great Sea. This is a time of patience, of waiting.

The Challenge

As the ultimate goals are in your grasp, you will find greatest satisfaction from helping your Fellows. Will you inspire and cajole them to greater efforts? Will they do the same for you? Have you found the one who will be your partner? There are times when the greatest gift is to not be there when needed most. Have they the self-sufficiency to overcome obstacles and use their own inspiration and courage? The moment of greatest gain can also be one of huge loss. Will you transcend those barriers? Can you lose yourself in the Work for the greater good? Will you know those moments when inaction is superior to action?

Part 11. General Exordium

The Breaking forth of the Light:

All these are in the Knowledge of Tho-oth.

The Assessors

Kurgiasax: Now then the Father of all issued as a mighty Wheel; the Sphinx, and the dog-headed god Typhon, were bound on his circumference.

Temphioth: Also came forth another Earth with her son, even Sekhet, the lady of Asi.

The Vision

An outpouring of Light from the Pole Star flows down. You project to a point outside the Earth, and you see the Earth spinning around the North Pole as if a Great Wheel, moved by the Sphinx, Typhon and a Man. The vision recedes, and you find yourself accompanied by Thoth, holding the Book of Tarot. Beside you is a tomb. It is empty inside. The inscription says it is the Tomb of Christian Rozenkreutz. You have passed the Valley of Death, you are reborn. Thoth turns the pages of the Book of Tarot. You see your mission, to guide lost souls to the Light.

The Challenge

The need for signs, evidence will have long past for you, but now you need to produce them for the Followers who waiver. Mask the serious with frivolity. The Fool will sieve out those who are unworthy. Your spiritual powers bring you choices. Will you influence politics? Will you work tirelessly for the New Aeon? Will you work with the Powers of Nature for knowledge?

The 22 Mercurial Spirits of Liber 231

For some reason Crowley chose to represent the names of these twenty-two spirits using a mixture of English, Greek and Coptic letters – the Hebrew alphabet is represented by AYN, or Nothingness, related to the Devil card. From the English letters the names of various Enochian, Goetic and other spirits can be discerned. The Coptic ST is explained in various Golden Dawn documents as having spiritualising influence from Kether. This leaves the Greek letters, which could have as easily been rendered in English. What do the Greek letters represent?

In my meditations on these Spirits, I was gradually led to consider Gnosis or Knowledge, usually secret knowledge. The Gnostics were on the one hand considered to be the precursors to the Christian religion, and on the other an enemy that had to be crushed by established religion. This philosophy was explored by Madame Blavatsky and the Theosophical Movement she founded. Alistair Crowley makes it clear in several places that he intended to continue the works of the Theosophical Movement, who, no doubt, feel they can get on quite nicely without his help. A characteristic of Gnosticism as it has come down to us is that its ideas have appropriated and misappropriated over the millennia. One side of Mercury that is not so well known is his role as thief. He steals things, ideas, and words. Spiritually, our original identity can and has been stolen. To know is to be.

"Basically, gnostics believe that we as humans are "outsiders" to this material universe. Our immortal godlike souls were trapped here in a body by evil forces, and we are reincarnated continually, while our true spiritual identities are clouded from our memory. It is our task to discover the hidden knowledge, or gnosis, that will allow us to escape this evil material world of illusion and return to our rightful place. We

keep reincarnating until we learn how to escape."
Jeff Jacobsen - The Hubbard is Bare (online document)

The other set of spirits, Amprodius, etc are described as Qliphotic, forces
that are 'outside' the Tree of Life, while this set of spirits are Mercurial. Could
the Mercurial spirits be the jailers? As a tarot reader, I firmly believe that as well
presenting problems in the life of the querent, the Tarot invariably will provide a
solution whether or not it is appreciated by the diviner or querent. In the twilight
world of spirits nothing is ever what it seems. If we see the 44 spirits of *Liber
231* as somehow conspiring to theft and imprisonment, a fate that is terrible to
the rational mind, but in the context of the Supernal Triangle there is often an
inversion of forces. In the Supernal view of Liber 231, the spirits hold the keys to
liberation and contact with one's Holy Guardian Angel either through ritual or
magical practice.

Here the reader may be reminded of Crowley's analysis of the court cards that
appears in the chapter on the Fool card in the Book of Thoth:

> *It is necessary, in order to understand the Tarot, to go back in history to the
> Matriarchal (and exogamic) Age, to the time when succession was not through the
> first-born son of the King, but through his daughter... In the most stable dynasties,
> the new king was always a stranger, a foreigner; what is more, he had to kill the old
> king and marry that king's daughter.*
> *Aleiseter Crowley, Book of Thoth*

Later, Crowley says:

> *"To ensure the succession, it was therefore devised: firstly, that the blood royal should
> really be the royal blood, and secondly, that this strain should be fortified by the
> introduction of the conquering stranger, instead of being attenuated by continual
> in-breeding.*
> *Aleiseter Crowley, Book of Thoth*

The nature of the Quest to find one's real nature requires long journeys,
possibly through foreign or alien philosophies until the realisation that the True
Self was already there at the start. In my own experience I have seen many spirits
who are angry, violent, and particularly dangerous, but since they have to be dealt
with by whatever means appropriate, I have found that either I have to incorporate
them into my self (this is a dangerous practice, not recommended unless the
magician is particularly experienced), whereupon the problem disappears, or as
in the Arabian Nights, the Spirit suddenly takes on a more benign form. Either

way, I experience an increase in knowledge or insight into a particular situation – real treasure from the spirits. Liberation is reciprocal – however alien they seem to us (and quite possibly us to them) – for spirits and for humans. It is but a short step to introduce aliens and UFOs to the discussion, for which in particular read Kenneth Grant's books.

Writers such as Kenneth Grant mention Crowley's Egyptian Gnosis without ever describing what this means. For Crowley, the Theosophical Society would have been the prime source of Gnosticism, particularly the writings of G.R.S. Mead. In his translation of the *Pistis Sophia, I, lxii,* there is a description of IAO where each letter has to be repeated three times:

> *Now these are the names which I will give from the Boundless onward. Write them with a sign, that the Sons of God may be revealed from here on.*
> *This is the name of the Immortal: _____, ____; and this the name of the Voice, for the sake of which the Perfect Man has set himself in motion: ____*
> G.R.S. Mead, *Pistis Sophia*

The quotation continues with various combinations of letters, all in groups of three, which is reflected in some of the names of the spirits. Now of course, we can see the groups of three letters as reflecting the influence of AYN SVP AVR, which has been considered in the book. In the Gnosis of the Mind:

> *... in the Trismegistic sermons, in which the disciple is reborn, or born in the Mind, he is all amazed that his "father" and initiator here below should remain there before him just as he ever was in his familiar form, while the efficacious rite is perfected by his means. The "father" of this "son" is the link, the channel of Gnosis; the true initiation is performed by the Great Initiator, the Mind.*
> G.R.S. Mead, *Gnosis of the Mind*

In a later paragraph Mead describes the function of the father:

> *"The office of the "father" is to bring the "son" to union with himself, so that he may be born out of ignorance into Gnosis, born in Mind, his Highest Self, and so become Son of the Father indeed."*
> G.R.S. Mead, *Gnosis of the Mind*

Mead aptly sums up the Divine Triad, incidentally giving a clue as to one origin of the concept of Dialectic found in Elemental Dignities:

> *It therefore follows that he who would be Gnostic, must not foolishly divorce within*

himself the mystery of the triple Partners, the Three Powers, or the Divine Triad. For him the object of his endeavour is to consummate the Sacred Marriage within himself, where Three must "marry" to create; that so he may be united to his Greatest Self and become at-one with God. Body, soul, and mind (or spirit, for in this Gnosis spirit is frequently a synonym of mind) must all work together in intimate union for righteousness.

G.R.S. Mead, *Gnosis of the Mind*

The Qliphot and the Tarot

The Meditations were written before my own understanding had increased to the point that they can be seen in a Gnostic context, but when included with the Mnemonic verses and verses of Liber 231, there is the basis for seeing the Tarot in a Gnostic Light. The Spirits discussed in this book are often considered to be Qliphotic, which is representing unbalanced, therefore dangerous or demonic energies that the magician should avoid until he has achieved high status and competency. The concept of the Qliphotic spirits comes from various Kabbalistic sources. The Qlippoth are never really explained, and it certainly was not the intention of the author to rashly introduce them to the readership. My experience of 'Qliphotic' Goetia and Liber 231 has been one of unending joy, a far cry from the terrifying descriptions given by writers down the centuries. I have been practising magic and divination for many years, so I tend to believe my own experience. If they are not evil, what are they? The answer seems to lie in Egyptian mythology, since that is the basis of the Golden Dawn rituals, as discussed in Chapter 11. The Bible and Kabbalah are based upon Egyptian mythology, a subject extensively discussed in Theosophy. According to the Egyptologist Gerald Massey, who was also a Theosophist, the Qliphoth were victims of Rabbinical spin!

> *It is also represented in the Rabbinical writings that the souls of the Israelites has a higher origin than the souls of the Gentiles. The souls of the Goim, they say, have their origin from the external powers, the power of klippoth or the demons, whereas the souls of the Israelites are derived from the Holy Spirit.*
> *Ancient Egypt in the Light of the World, Massey, 1907*

Massey's central thesis is that the Old and New Testaments are entirely based upon the Egyptian Mysteries, so for the Rabbis to declare Qliphotic Spirits to be evil is akin to the practice of medieval mapmakers to write 'here be dragons' on unknown areas. Explicitly and implicitly, the Spirits of Liber 231 are founded upon Egyptian principles, so why did Aleister Crowley describe one set of the spirits as Qliphotic?

The derivation of Qlippoth QLYPVTh is supposed to be "shells", plural, and the appendage VTh on any Hebrew word denotes plurality. Most Hebrew words have three letter roots, and this is where the problem starts, because Qlippoth does not appear in the Old Testament, and there does not seem to be a word for "shell"! QLI means 'roasted grain", not much help, but QLL means to be small, light, to be lessened, to be despised, and to curse – in other words something trivial or inconsequential. QLO is a sling, or something to swing. If we spell the word with a K, KLA means to imprison or confine, while KLH is to complete, to finish, to destroy. Again, there is no root KLP. From this approach, the Rabbis may have wanted to minimise the importance of these spirits, continuing a well known tradition of demonising the Gods of the previous regime. So, we have a horde of unnamed spirits, who have no basis in Hebrew gematria, who have been demonised. It is also interesting to note that the Qlippoth are associated with spirits in the Garden of Eden, which Gerald Massey equates to Amenta, the abode of the Dead found in the Egyptian Book of the Dead.

QLYPVTh = 626, a number that has only OShRYN, the tenth portion, which suggests that Kabbalists were consciously trying to minimise the influence of eleven. Removing VTh, we have 220, which is immeasurably more interesting. There are 220 verses in the Book of the Law, which provides another link between Liber AL and the Book of Thoth. The Elect, clean, elegant, and Giants are other equivalent words. 221 is associated with the Swastika, which of course appears in several of the symbols in Liber 231.

The commonly used word for Qlippoth is 'husk', ZG, the skin of a grape, which apart from numerating as 10, has no particular significance. KLYPVTh = 546, equated with MThVQ, sweet, and ShVMR, a watchman, and ShMVR, Custodi. In the singular, we have 140, which is the number of MLKYM, Kings, Angels of Tipareth of Assiah, and of Netzach of Briah. The association with Tipareth which points to 66: "The Mystic Number of the Qliphoth, and of the Great Work (Liber 777). In English Qabalah (EQ) 'us' is 66, which brings to mind:

My number is 11, as all their numbers who are of us. The Five Pointed Star, with a Circle in the Middle, & the circle is Red. My colour is black to the blind, but the blue

and gold are seen of the seeing. Also I have a secret glory for them that love me.
Aleister Crowley, Liber AL 1. 60

The Bible also makes significant use of 'us':

God said, 'Let us make man in our image, in the likeness of ourselves, and let them
be masters of the fish of the sea, the birds of heaven, the cattle, all the wild beasts
and all the reptiles that crawl upon the earth.
Genesis 1. 26

The pretence of a Single God causes all kinds of problems for translators and theologians alike, since it is the ALHYM or Gods who are speaking at this point. The number 86 is discussed at the beginning of Chapter 6, which concerns Tipareth, the point of contact for the Holy Guardian Angel. The Great Work of course is concerned with conversations with one's Holy Guardian Angel. 66 is the summation of the numbers 1 to 11. Far from being demonic, the use of the Mystic and the Great Work points to a profound system of magick. This is made clear by the word GLGL, a wheel, seen in the Fortune card and hence the Wheel of Tarot.

Shell refers to the shattering of the first vessels on the Tree of Life before they were rectified (Tikkun) to produce the Sephiroth we know today.

If the Qlippoth or Shells are so evil, why emphasise the connection to the Torah? The question runs deeper when one looks at the Kings of Edom (Genesis 36), who are explicitly associated with the Shells. The Bible says nothing derogatory about the Kings, apart from the fact that they are from the line of Esau, merely listing them. Edom is ADVM, which is Adam without the V, and V is of course 6, relating to Tipareth. The gematria of 51 produces ate, devoured, pain, to harass, perturb, and failure: all these point to something terribly wrong. However, the final M as 600 produces 611, ThVRH, the Torah! The Bible makes it clear that '*Esau is Edom' Genesis 36. 8*. Esau, OSHV is 376, the number of Shalom, peace, a bird, and also 'dominator'; again there is little here to see as 'evil' in any way.

Eleven is the One beyond Ten, usually considered as Daath on the Tree of Life, but if instead of externalising the Tree of Life, then One beyond Ten can be seen as One beyond the Self, which is one way of describing the Holy Guardian Angel. Tipareth as 6 is the point of the Tree of Life where contact with the Holy Guardian Angel is made, so in combination with 11, we have the overturning of the self to attain the Self.

Finally, there is a 42 Lettered Name of God, which consists of a string of 42 Hebrew letters. Qabalists are silent as to the nature or origins of this name, but in the nature of this discussion, it is easy to see that it may have something to do with the first names of the 42 Assessors. It may be significant that 42 is the number of YVD HH VV, the three consonants in YHVH. It is also the number of AMA, Mother, a title of Binah.

Theosophy and the Golden Dawn are two halves of the same coin. Mathers, Yeats and other influential members of the Golden Dawn were Theosophists, while Crowley stated in several places that he intended to carry on the work of Theosophy. No doubt the title Book of Thoth is entirely appropriate.

Self Initiation and the Neophyte Spread

In this more egalitarian world, the necessity to be at a Temple, or even be a member of a Lodge in order to progress spiritually has waned. Cyber-Temples can be found on the Internet. With the development of the powerful magical techniques for attaining one's Holy Guardian Angel using the Tarot, a more formal structure for self-initiation is required.

Contact with one's Holy Guardian Angel is considered a pre-requisite for any Magician – Aleister Crowley purchased Boleskin in Scotland purely for the purpose of practising the Abra-Melin ritual. Six months of isolation and abstinence is required to complete the Abra-Melin ritual – not an easy task at the best of times.

A characteristic of success in contacting one's Holy Guardian Angel is the appearance of 'demonic' spirits. The word demon comes from daimon, a Greek word meaning deity, something entirely different. Based upon my experience of writing this book and the contact made with the Goetic Spirits, (which are part of the Abra-Melin heritage) and the spirits of Liber 231, it occurs to me that 'demon' in this context may better be described as 'spirits who arrived unexpectedly'.

Now of course, some care has to be taken with this approach since they could well be demonic in the accepted meaning of the word. The Golden Dawn system developed magical techniques to test any spirit that appeared and to ensure the spirit departed at the behest of the magician. In any kind of magical and spiritual work the Magician should be well acquainted with these techniques. The author does not claim any adepthood since he has never been a member of any Lodge system, and the appearance of the spirits during the writing of this book needs to be seen in the context of magical and shamanic work that has formed the basis of his life since a teenager.

The techniques and methods in this book have illuminated the distinct possibility that Tarot has a more fundamental underpinning of the Golden Dawn system that goes beyond the attributions to the Tree of Life and Grade Rituals. The primary goal for the Magician is contact with one's Holy Guardian Angel, and it is clear that the Opening of the Key Spread was used by Adepts within the Golden Dawn for this purpose. Now tarot readers and magicians alike can benefit from these techniques. Of course, competency in Counting and Pairing and the ability to identify the Unaspected cards is no guarantee that spirits will appear to the Diviner, unbidden or not. As all books on magic testify, preparation and practice and hard work are the foundation of any magical success.

The structure of this book can be seen entirely as a manual for self-initiation. Now of course as I discussed in the Introduction, the division of eleven chapters and the meditation on pairing the Major Cards at the beginning of each chapter was an editorial decision made at the book's inception. However, when one works in accordance with the spirit of tarot, both literally and metaphorically, tarot has an incredible power of re-organisation.

The integration of the Paired Major cards at the beginning of the chapter and the Spirits of Liber 231 described in the Appendices can be seen as the basis of study and work for self-initiation. For the Goetic Spirits the Bornless Ritual is recommended. The Bornless Ritual begins:

> *Thee I invoke, the Bornless one.*
> *Thee, that didst create the Earth and the Heavens:*
> *Thee, that didst create the Night and the Day.*
> *Thee, that didst create the Darkness and the Light.*
> *Thou art Osorronophris: Whom no man hath seen at any time.*
> *Thou art Jabas:*
> *Thou art Iapos:*
> *Thou has distinguished between the just and the unjust.*
> *Thou didst make the female and the male.*
> *Thou didst produce the Seed and the Fruit.*
> *Thou didst form Men to love one another, and to hate one another.*

Preparing the Sacred Space

A dedicated private area that can be maintained in your home or a place for a period of months is recommended. Failing that, the aspirant will have to establish and purify the Altar each time it is set up. However you arrange your sacred space, you will be regularly purifying and invoking the room. The Altar should be big enough to spread the cards out. You should use any accepted methods of purification that you are comfortable with, such as found in the Golden Dawn, Wicca or Shamanism. The same applies to the magical or ritual instruments you place on the altar.

To facilitate the process I recommend purchasing a dedicated tarot deck purely for the purpose of self-initiation – the Thoth Tarot is particularly suited. In a ritual setting, place the Tarot deck on your altar and recite:

> *"I invoke Thee, HUA, the Great Angel who art set over the operations of this secret Wisdom, to strengthen and establish [Name or Magical Name] in my search for the Mysteries of the Divine Light. Increase my Spiritual perception and enable me to rise beyond that lower Self-hood which is nothing, unto that Highest Self-hood which is God the Vast One."*
>
> *Adapted from "The Consecration Ceremony of the Vault of the Adepti"*

Alternatively, you may use the invocation found in the Opening of the Key instructions, and found in the Book of Thoth.

Take the cards in your left hand. In the right hand hold the wand over them, and say:

> *I invoke thee IAO, that thou wilt send HRU, the great Angel that is set over the operations of this Secret Wisdom, to lay his hand invisibly upon these consecrated cards of art, that thereby we may obtain true knowledge of hidden things, to the glory of thine ineffable Name. Amen.*

Recite the General Exordium:

1. The Speech in the Silence:
2. The Words against the Son of Night:
3. The Voice of Thoth before the Universe in the presence of the eternal Gods:
4. The Formulas of Knowledge:
5. The Wisdom of Breath:
6. The Radix of Vibration:
7. The Shaking of the Invisible:
8. The Rolling Asunder of the Darkness:
9. The Becoming Visible of Matter:
10. The Piercing of the Coils of the Stooping Dragon:
11. The Breaking forth of the Light:
    All these are in the Knowledge of Tho-oth.

Recite all or part of the Bornless Ritual.

The Tarot deck will remain on the Altar for the entire period of the Self-initiation.

Self-Initiation Program

The Abra-Melin book recommends six months, but a better structure to work within is a multiple of eleven, such as eleven weeks or eleven months. A crash program of eleven days is not recommended except in extreme emergencies – and the author takes no responsibility for such a course of action.

At the start of the first period, after the purification and invocation of the Great Angel HUA, take the Fool and Universe cards from the tarot deck. Place them either side of the deck on the altar. You may wish to prop them up so you can contemplate them while you study and meditate. You will have already studied the attributions of these cards from the *Golden Dawn, Liber 777* or Dion Fortune's *Mystical Qabalah*. By placing the remaining 76 cards between the two Major cards you are ensuring that none of the other cards are ignored. You may wish to use the names of the spirits of Liber 231 in your invocation – there are no pronunciation guidelines for the Mercurial Spirits, so do your best – they know who they are, and appreciate the effort put in by the magician. You may also include the Kabbalistic Holy Names associated with the Hebrew letters of the respective cards. Study and analyse the Gematria of the combination of the two Major cards. Meditate on the General Exordium and the Bornless Ritual.

At the end of each Period, perform a banishing ritual. Ritually place the two cards back into the deck and then put the next two cards on the altar (i.e., the Magus and Aeon for the second week or month).

Extending the practise of Self-initiation

The above is an example of the bare bones of the self-initiation program. In addition to the meditation on each pair of cards each week or month, the Magician may perform a ritual divination using the first stage of the Opening of the Key Spread. Instead of fanning out one of the piles in a horseshoe, all four piles of cards will be fanned out on the altar and left in situ for the full period of one week or month, or for the full eleven periods. During this time, study and analyse the cards using the techniques described in this book, identifying in particular all the Unaspected cards. Put extra study on the spirits represented by the Unaspected cards. Take note of any predictions made in the cards and see how the predictions manifest in your life.

Another variation is to use a modified Neophyte Spread whereby two columns of the paired Major cards are laid out. The remainder of the deck is shuffled and five cards are dealt out between each pair. The final card represents Zero, and will have some bearing on what the Magician can expect during the period of the ritual. The spread will remain on the altar for the full period or eleven periods as determined by the magician. Analysis of the spread will proceed as below.

Determining the success or otherwise of Self-initiation is difficult. At the least, one's knowledge of the Tarot and how it relates to one's life will be immeasurably strengthened. Be aware that the appearance of the Spirits can happen at any time of the day or night, in waking, dreaming or sleeping, at places other than the Altar. For myself, the names of the Spirits came into my head, and later some of the Goetic spirits appeared looking as described in the various Goetic manuals available. As much as possible, the Magician should maintain a normal lifestyle.

Initiation in a Group or Lodge

Knowing whether or not a candidate will be suitable for a Lodge or Esoteric group has always been an inexact science. The schisms in the Golden Dawn are a good example of the failure to predict success or otherwise of the Candidate in the group. Traditionally, the natal horoscope has been used, but with the Neophyte Spread, Officers now have an extra tool. For example, the position of the 9 or 10 Swords could indicate at what level the candidate would experience greatest mental stress. Excess of an inimical element at a particular Degree would also show problems.

The Neophyte Spread

Basic Form

The cards are dealt out into eleven piles (modules) of seven cards. This can be done either by counting seven cards for module 1, then seven for module 2, and so on, or by laying down a single card on each of the eleven modules, building them up in sequence. There will be one card left, which is the Fool position, and can appear either at the beginning or the end of the spread, or can be seen outside the spread. Some experimentation needs to be done on this.

Once the top cards have been analysed, each pile is opened up, spread out and analysed using Card Counting and Pairing. The 78th card can be analysed in relationship to each Module using Elemental Dignities. For those who prefer a more structured approach, each sequence of seven cards can be associated with the seven planets. There are several ways of ordering the planets either from right to left, or left to right, and it is important that whatever order is used, the reader is consistent. If the first card is Mars, then the first card in every Module is associated with Mars. Since eleven is the number of change, not just for Aleister Crowley, but also the Golden Dawn, if a ritual was considered for the transformation of Mars, then a thorough analysis of the Martial cards such as 2 Wands, the Tower, Death card etc would be undertaken.

The eleven stacks correspond to the eleven lines of the General Exordium, which is the fundamental structure of Golden Dawn ritual, particularly the Neophyte 0=0 ritual which is the basis of the magical rituals, including divination.

General Exordium

In commenting upon the General Exordium, Pat Zalewski says:

> *"The general meaning of the above verse relates to the Great Thoth, the highest aspect*
> *of the Hermes of the most ancient Egyptian Mysteries, and corresponds almost to*
> *the Great Angel Metatron. It is the Archangel of Kether in the Briatic World."*
> *Pat Zalewksi, Z1 Golden Dawn Rituals, Llewellyn.*

Knowledge in the rituals of the Golden Dawn, particularly the 0=0 Neophyte ritual is helpful, and I would direct the reader to Pat Zalewski's excellent series of books on the Z5 Secret Teachings of the Golden Dawn. Having said that, the commentary on the Meditations and Liber 231 in the appendices gives the reader an excellent overview of what the Module is about. The versatility of the 0=0 Neophyte ritual is reflected in the versatility of the Neophyte spread.

The reason I have used the term 'Module' rather than position is that although the Piles of cards are read in sequence, the layout or pattern of the eleven Modules will depend on the nature and structure of the divination.

A fundamental aspect of the Neophyte spread is the 'Mystical circumambulation' where there is a procession around the double cubed Altar which creates a spiral or vortex of energy. This vortex can be replicated in the Neophyte spread where a clockwise spiral layout is used to draw down spiritual energy, while an anticlockwise spiral is used to disperse spiritual energy.

The starting point of the Neophyte Spread could be one of the four elements, in which case the position of the first Module would be in the cardinal direction from the Altar.

The seven cards in each unit are laid out in the form an arrow:

1. Pillar of Severity, Binah, Antithesis
2. card
3. card
4. Middle Pillar, Synthesis

5.   card
6.   card
7.   Pillar of Mercy, Chokmah, Thesis

The direction of the arrow points to the next unit in the chain. The layout of the units will depend on the nature or reading contemplated. The simplest form of the reading will create a vertical column starting from the bottom, working up to the top. Since the mystical circumambulation is an intrinsic part of the ceremony, the units can be laid out in a spiral form, based upon on the cosmic cube. The direction of the spiral will depend on the nature of the ritual: clockwise for invoking and manifesting, and anticlockwise for banishing or removing. There are many permutations based upon the starting point, but first, here is what the Golden Dawn says on the subject:

> *"In the Ritual of the Enterer are shadowed forth symbolically, the beginning of certain of the Formulae of the Magic of Light. For this Ritual, betokeneth a certain Person, Substance or Thing, which is taken from the dark World of Matter, to be brought under the operation of the Divine Formulae of the Magic of Light."*
> Israel Regardie, The Golden Dawn

There are five classes according to YHShVH:

Yod or Fire: Ceremonial Magic – Evocations of the Spirits of the Elements
Heh or Water: Consecration and charging of Telesmata, and the production of
    Natural Phenomena such as storms, earthquakes, etc.
Shin or Spirit: Spiritual development, transformations, invisibility
Vau or Air: Divination of all types. The art of making the Link between the
    subject of the work and process of divination.
Heh or Earth: Alchemical works, Transmutation

The Golden Dawn gives examples of these five classes, based upon the 0=0 Ceremony in 24 steps, but as Pat Zalewski demonstrates, there are actually eleven stages based upon the General Exordium. That nature of each unit in the reading is discussed in the analysis of the paired Major cards, and the verses of Liber 231 at the beginning of each chapter of this book. We can also consider the first and last card of each group of seven cards as representing the same paired cards.

The Golden Dawn elemental attributions for the directions are: 1. North, Air, 2. East, Fire, 3. South, Earth, 4. West, Water

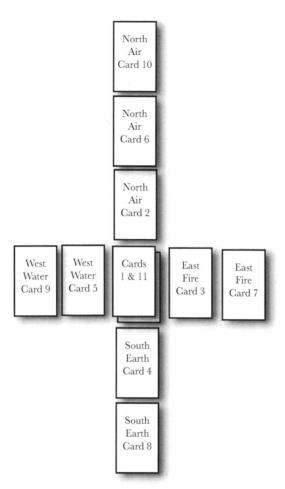

For a divination commencing with North, Air (this would concern anything to do with Divination), after two circuits, we arrive back at North with unit 10, and then we can return to the Centre, which is analogous to the Altar. With this method, there are echoes of the Celtic Cross spread, which has two cards, "above and below".

BIBLIOGRAPHY

Blavatsky, H.P. *The Secret Doctrine,* Theosophical Society
Cook & Hawk, *Shamanism & the Esoteric Tradition,* 1992 Llewellyn
Crowley, Aleister *Book of Thoth* 1944 Weiser
Crowley, Aleister *Liber 777* 1973 Weiser
Crowley, Aleister *Book IV, Magic* Weiser
Crowley, Aleister *The Vision & the Voice* Weiser
Crowley, Aleister *The Book of the Law* 1904
Crowley, Aleister *The Book of Lies* 1913 Weiser
Crowley, Aleister *Liber 231*
Crowley, Aleister *Konx Om Pax* 1907
Crowley, Aleister *The Wake World* 1907
Crowley, Aleister *The Sword of the Song* 1904
Denning, Melitta & Phillips, Osborne *Mysteria Magica* 1988 Llewellyn
DuQuette, Lon Milo *Tarot of Ceremonial Magick* 1995 Weiser
DuQuette, Lon Milo *Aleister Crowley's Illustrated Goetia* 1992 New Falcon Publicatic
Eliade, Mircea *Shamanism* 1989 Arkana
Falorio, Linda *Shadow Tarot* 1995 Headless Press
Fortune, Dion *The Circuit of Force* Thoth
Fortune, Dion *Principles of Hermetic Philosophy* Thoth
Fortune, Dion *An Introduction to Ritual Magic* Thoth
Fortune, Dion *The Mystical Qabalah* 1935
Grant, Kenneth *Nightside of Eden* 1994 Skoob Books
Greer, Mary *Women of the Golden Dawn* 1995 Park Street Press
Johnson, Josephine *Florence Farr* 1975 Colin Smythe Ltd
Kaplan, Aryeh *Sepher Yetsirah* 1991 Weiser
Kaplan, Aryeh *Meditation and Kabbalah* 1982 Weiser
Kraig, Donald Michael *Tarot & Magic* 2002 Llewellyn
Kraig, Donald Michael *Modern Magick* Llewellyn
Kraig, Donald Michael *Sex Magick* Llewellyn
Küntz, Darcy *The Complete Golden Dawn Manuscript* 1996 Holmes

Küntz, Darcy *The Golden Dawn Tarot - A.E. Waite* 1996 Holmes

Küntz, Darcy *The Enochian Experiments of the Golden Dawn* 1996 Holmes

Levi, Eliphas *Transcendental Magic* 1995 Bracken

MacGregor, Mathers S.L. *The Kabbalah Unveiled* 1970 Routledge

MacGregor, Mathers S.L. *The Key of Solomon the King* 1974 Weiser

Papus *Tarot of the Bohemians* Melvin Powers

Raine, Kathleen *Yeats, the Tarot and the Golden Dawn* 1972 Dolmen

Regardie, Israel *Golden Dawn Book* 1971 Llewellyn

Regardie, Israel *The Tree of Life* 2001 Llewellyn

Regardie, Israel *A Garden of Pomegranates* 1970 Llewellyn

Regardie, Israel *The Eye in the Triangle* Llewellyn

Reuss, Theodor & Crowley, Aleister *O.T.O. Rituals and Sex Magick* 1999 I-H-O Books

Wallis-Budge, E.A. *The Book of the Dead* 1909 Routledge

Zalewski, Pat *Secret Inner Order Rituals of the Golden Dawn* 1988 Falcon

Zalewski Pat & Zalewski, Chris *The Equinox & Solstice Ceremonies of the Golden Dawn* 1992 Llewellyn